ACE THE PENNSYLVANIA NOTARY PUBLIC EXAM

Notary Public Law + Legal Highlights

225 Questions + 2 Practice Exams

Angelo Tropea

ACE THE PENNSYLVANIA NOTARY PUBLIC EXAM

Copyright 2018 by Angelo Tropea. All rights reserved. Unless permitted by U.S. copyright law, no part of this book may be reproduced in any form or by any electronic or mechanical means, without permission in writing from the publisher.

ISBN 13: 978-1721730100
ISBN 10: 1721730109

The unofficial sections of laws and accompanying "highlights" are edited and are presented solely for the purpose of quick study aids and not as legal reference. The primary sources of legal reference are the laws and regulations themselves which are available for free in many places, including online.

> "Notaries Public…hold an office which can trace its origins back to ancient Rome when they were called *scribae, tabellius* or *notarius*. They are easily the oldest continuing branch of the legal profession worldwide."

CONTENTS

1. THE AIM OF THIS BOOK / 4

2. HOW TO USE THIS BOOK / 5

3. LIST OF LAWS AND REGULATIONS / 6

4. HOW TO BECOME A NOTARY PUBLIC / 10

5. NOTARY PUBLIC LAW & HIGHLIGHTS / 21

6. RULONA LAW & HIGHLIGHTS / 46

7. NOTARY OMNIBUS AMENDMENTS / 120

8. UNIFORM ACKNOWLEDGMENT ACT / 126

9. RULONA REGULATIONS / 136

10. LEGAL TERMS / 157

11. NOTARY PUBLIC FEES / 161

12. QUICK QUESTIONS / 163

13. MULTIPLE CHOICE QUESTIONS / 221

14. PRACTICE EXAMS
    EXAM 1 QUESTIONS / 275
    EXAM 1 ANSWERS / 281

    EXAM 2 QUESTIONS / 282
    EXAM 2 ANSWERS / 288

THE AIM OF THIS BOOK

In Pennsylvania there are approximately 85,000 notaries public, all appointed and commissioned by the Pennsylvania Department of State. The Department maintains an excellent website that provides all the information you need on notary public matters, including application procedure, administrative regulations and relevant laws. It contains the text of sections of law and regulations that you need to pass the Notary Public Exam and to be a well informed and professional notary public. The aim of this book is to complement the laws and regulations by highlighting the more important facts and offering study tools to help you better prepare for the exam and become a more knowledgeable and professional practicing notary public.

THIS BOOK PROVIDES

1. Edited sections of Pennsylvania laws and regulations on the scope of the Notary Public Exam.
2. Law highlights to stress and clarify legal facts and areas that are most relevant to notary public candidates.
3. True/False, Fill-in and other "Quick Questions" to help you remember facts and legal terms.
4. Multiple-choice questions to help you practice for the notary public exam.
5. Practice exams to help you to further strengthen your knowledge of the laws relevant to notaries.

We believe that the combination of the above study tools will provide the required practice to help you achieve your goal of passing the notary public exam and also increase your understanding and appreciation of laws important to notaries public.

HOW TO USE THIS BOOK

There are probably as many ways to study successfully as there are people. However, in the more than thirty years preparing study materials and conducting classes for civil service exams, I have found that certain methods seem to work better than others with the great majority of students. The following are time tested suggestions that you might want to consider as you incorporate this book in the study plan that is best for you.

SUGGESTIONS

1. First read the law highlights. They highlight important facts and are generally in simpler English than the edited statutes.
2. After reading the highlights, read the edited statutes for a deeper understanding. (The statutes are unofficial and edited in places.)
3. Try the "Quick Questions" (5 on a page). Do not go on to the multiple-choice questions until you have mastered these questions. Read the comments after the answers to reinforce important facts.
4. Now tackle the multiple-choice questions (3 on page). On the actual test you will have around 30 multiple-choice questions.
5. When you think you are ready, take Practice Test 1, then Practice Test 2.

Whenever you answer a question incorrectly, review that section of law or regulations. Also, make sure you are confident with all the legal terms. They will form the basis of your understanding of the law. Study every day. Take this book with you – and make it your friend.

The actual law is available for free in many places, including online at:
http://www.dos.pa.gov/OtherServices/Notaries/Resources/Pages/Laws-.aspx

ACE THE PENNSYLVANIA NOTARY PUBLIC EXAM

The Notary Public Law (Jul. 1, 2003)

Section	Description and Page Number
1	Short Title / 22
2	Appointment of Notaries / 22
3	Eligibility / 22
4	Disqualification; Exception / 22
5	Application to Become a Notary Public / 24
6	Application for Reappointment / 26
7	Vacation of Office / 26
8	Oath of Office; Bond; Recording / 28
9	Registration of Notary's Signature; Fee / 30
10	Change of Name / 30
11	Refund of Fee (Repealed June 30, 1888) / 32
12	Notarial Seal / 32
13	Date of Expiration of Commission (Repealed 6/30/1988) / 36
14	Position of Seal and Date of Expiration of Commission (Repealed June 30, 1988) / 36
15	Register; Copies of Records / 36
16	Power to Administer Oaths and Affirmations / 38
17	Power to take Acknowledgment of Instruments of Writing Relating to Commerce or Navigation and to Make Declarations (Repealed by 2002) / 38
18	Power to Take Depositions, Affidavits and Acknowledgment of Writings Relative to Lands (Repealed 2002, Dec. 9) / 38

19	Limitations on Powers; Fees / 38
20	Admissibility in Evidence (Repealed April 28, 1978) / 40
21	Fees of Notaries Public / 40
22	Rejection of Application; Removal / 40
22.1	Surrender of Seal / 42
22.2	Revocation of Commission for Certain Personal Checks / 42
22.3	Regulations / 44
23	Specific Repeal / 44
24	Repeals / 44

Pennsylvania's Revised Uniform Law on Notarial Acts (RULONA: effective October 26, 2017)

Section	Description and Page Number
301	Short title of chapter / 46
302	Definitions / 46
303	Applicability / 52
304	Authority to perform notarial act / 54
305	Requirements for certain notarial acts / 54
306	Personal appearance required / 56
307	Identification of individual / 58
308	Authority to refuse to perform notarial act / 60
309	Signature if individual unable to sign (Reserved) / 60

310	Notarial act in this Commonwealth / 60
311	Notarial act in another state / 64
312	Notarial act under authority of federally recognized Indian tribe / 64
313	Notarial act under federal authority / 66
314	Foreign notarial act / 68
315	Certificate of notarial act / 72
316	Short form certificates / 76
317	Official stamp / 88
318	Stamping device / 88
319	Journal / 90
320	Notification regarding performance of notarial act on electronic record; selection of technology / 94
321	Appointment and commission as notary public; qualifications; no immunity or benefit / 96
322	Examination, basic education and continuing education / 102
323	Sanctions / 104
324	Database of notaries public / 108
325	Prohibited acts / 110
326	Validity of notarial acts / 112
327	Regulations / 114
328	Notary public commission in effect / 116
329	Savings clause / 116
329.1	Fees of notaries public / 118

330	Uniformity of application and construction / 118
331	Relation to electronic Signatures in Global and National Commerce Act / 118

NOTARIES PUBLIC (57 PA.C.S.) - OMNIBUS AMENDMENTS
Act of Jul. 9, 2014, P.L. 1035, No. 119   Cl. 57
Session of 2014

1 - 7.1	Omnibus Amendments / 120

UNIFORM ACKNOWLEDGMENT ACT(*)
(Act No. 188, approved July 24, 1941, as amended by Acts 353 and 354 of 1947, Act 3 of 1951, Act 58 of 1957, Act 61 of 1961 and Act 71 of 1981)

1 - 14	Types of Acknowledgments, Certificate Forms / 126

RULONA REGULATIONS - Proposed August 2016
Selected Sections

161.1 - 167.127	Selected sections / 136

Shortened notations used for simplicity

notary public or notarial officer = notary
Secretary of the Commonwealth = Secretary
The Department of State of the Commonwealth of
      Pennsylvania = department
he/she = he
chapter = law
("the" has been omitted whenever possible and "individual" and "person" are used interchangeably for simplicity, although their definitions differ.)

How to Become a Notary Public

The official website for Notary Information and Online Notary Public Application is:

www.notaries.pa.gov

The links on the website include the following:

1. Notary Information
   What is a Notary
   Notary Education Providers
   General Information and Equipment
   Laws

2. Online Application
   Online Notary Application & Reappointment
   Check New Application Status
   Update Notary Info
   Notary Searchable Database & eServices

   ENotary Services
     Application
     Check Status
     Select Vendors

3. Complaints

The website and its links are excellent and provide the information you need to know, including the following:

Eligibility requirements

Notaries public:

1. Must be at least 18 years old.
   Notaries are commissioned for 4 years from the date of appointment.

2. Must be a US citizen or permanent legal resident of the US.

3. Must be a resident of the Commonwealth (Pennsylvania) or have a place of employment or practice in the Commonwealth.
4. Must be able to read and write the English language.
5. Must not be disqualified because of any of the following 3 reasons:
    1. character
    2. criminal convictions
    3. prior legal sanctions
6. For appointment and reappointment, notaries must have successfully completed 3 hours of approved education within 6 months of appointment or reappointment.
7. New notary public applicants and applicants with expired commissions must pass an examination administered by Pearson VUE (the Department's authorized examination vendor).

RULONA Regulations 167.111. Notary Public Examination.

Examination results shall be valid for a period of one (1) year from the date of the examination.

An applicant must score 80%* or better to pass the examination.

An applicant may retake the examination within a six-month period as many times as necessary to pass. The maximum frequency with which the examination may be repeated is one time per 24-hour period.

* (Please consult current rules regarding all requirements.)

Requirements for a notary public to be issued a commission

1. Applicant must submit an application with a $42 fee

ACE THE PENNSYLVANIA NOTARY PUBLIC EXAM

and verification that he has the necessary honesty, integrity and reliability to act as a notary public.

2. Applicant must provide proof of completion of approved 3-hour course within past 6 months. Applicant must also state that he has not made any fraudulent, dishonest or deceitful misstatement or omission in the application.

3. Obtaining a passing grade on the notary public exam. (computerized test, 30 questions, 60 minutes to complete the exam, 75% "scaled score"* required for passing.)

4. Cannot have been convicted or accepted Accelerated Rehabilitative Disposition for felony or for offense that involved fraud, dishonesty, or deceit.

5. Cannot have finding against or liability admission or disciplinary action based on fraud, deceit or dishonesty.

6. Has never failed to do the duties of a notary public.

7. Has never used misleading or false advertising regarding notary public duties and rights.

8. Has not violated a regulation of the department.

9. Has never had a notary commission disciplined by the Commonwealth or any other state, or have a commission refused to renew, revoked, or suspended.

10. Has never failed to maintain a bond.

A notary public application may for good cause be rejected by the Secretary of the Commonwealth.

Lack of proof of completion of required 3-hour course will result in outright rejection and cannot be appealed.

* (Please consult current code and regulations for all current requirements.)

Who is not eligible to be a notary public?

1. a member of the US Congress
2. a Federal employee who receives salary, fees, or perquisites ("perks")
3. a member of the General Assembly of Pennsylvania

When a person is appointed a notary public, the Department of State sends to the person:

1. notice of appointment
2. bond and oath form (to be executed by the applicant)
3. processing instructions

Within 45 days from the date of appointment, the applicant must:

1. take oath of office and record his oath, completed bond, and commission.
   (This must be done in the Recorder of Deeds in the county where the business of the notary is located.)
2. register his signature with the Prothonotary's office. (This must also be done in the county where the business of the notary is located.)

Failure to complete the above two steps will result in the notary's commission becoming null and void. The individual will be required to reapply with a new application and a new fee.

For complete and current information, visit the official website:

www.notaries.pa.gov

What Powers Does a Notary Have?

1. Administer oaths and affirmations

> Examples:
>
> Notary: Do you solemnly swear (or affirm) that the statements contained in this affidavit are true to the best of your knowledge and belief?
>
> Affiant: I do.
>
> --
>
> Notary: Do you solemnly swear (or affirm) that the testimony that you are about to give will be the truth, the whole truth, and nothing but the truth?
>
> Witness: I do.

2. Take acknowledgments of a record
3. Take verifications of a statement on oath or affirmation
4. Witness or attest signatures

With regard to the above duties (1-4), a notary, based on personal knowledge and satisfactory evidence, is responsible for:
    1. confirming the identity of the person, and
    2. confirming that the signature on the record matches the signature of the person.

5. Certify copies or depositions
    Notary must determine that the copy is a complete and accurate reproduction.

6. Note protests of negotiable instruments.
    The notary must determine the matters set forth in 13 Pa.C.S. Section 3505(b) (evidence of dishonor).

Some Things a Notary Cannot Do

1. A notary <u>cannot</u> delegate his notarial authority to another person.

2. A notary <u>cannot</u> transfer his notary public commission.

3. A notary <u>cannot</u> allow his notary public commission to be used by another person.

4. A notary <u>cannot</u> allow his journal or stamping device to leave his control.

5. A notary <u>cannot</u> take an application for marriage, issue a marriage license, or conduct a civil marriage ceremony.

6. A notary <u>cannot</u> perform a notarial act if the notary or spouse have a pecuniary interest in the transaction.

7. A notary should not use his title (Notary Public) or rubber stamp seal or embosser to complete the I-9 form as an authorized representative of the employer.

8. A notary <u>cannot</u> notarize his own signature or statement or a spouse's signature or statement.

9. A notary <u>cannot</u> notarize records in blank or official documents such as birth and death records.

10. A notary <u>cannot</u> post-date or pre-date notarial acts.

11. A notary <u>cannot</u> alter a document after it has been notarized.

12. A notary <u>cannot</u> use his notarial seal as special authority to act as a bill collection agent.

13. A notary <u>cannot</u> notarize a rubber-stamped signature.

14. A notary <u>cannot</u> give legal advice or act as an attorney.

ACE THE PENNSYLVANIA NOTARY PUBLIC EXAM

15. A notary cannot put himself out as an expert on immigration matters or immigration consultant.

16. A notary cannot refuse to perform a notarial act for reasons that are discriminatory.

17. A notary cannot perform a notarial act outside the state of Pennsylvania.

18. A notary cannot use his stamp to promote any product.

19. A notary public who is not an attorney may not use the term "notario" or "notario publico.

20. A notary cannot certify a copy of US Citizenship Certificate.

Personal Knowledge and Satisfactory Evidence

Generally, the individual executing a signature or making a statement must appear personally before the notary. Also, the notary must have <u>satisfactory evidence or personal knowledge</u> of the identity of the individual.

Satisfactory evidence includes:
1. A passport
2. A driver's license or government-issued non-driver ID
3. Other government issued ID which meets all of these 3 requirements:
    1) The ID is current (expiration date has not passed).
    2) The ID has the signature or photograph of the person.
    3) The ID is satisfactory to the notary.
4. A verification on oath or affirmation by a witness who is personally known to the notary and who is appearing personally before the notary.

If a notary is <u>not</u> satisfied as to the identity or signature or other material fact, the notary may refuse to perform a notarial service.

However, a notary <u>cannot</u> refuse to perform a notarial act because of a person's race, religion, color, national origin, disability, marital status, sexual orientation, gender identity or pregnancy.

Notary Public Seal/Stamp and Journal

Official Seal

Notaries public must use an official seal for all acts, instruments and attestations. The rubber stamp seal for paper documents must be a maximum height of 1 inch and a width of 3 ½ inches with plain border.

It must contain, in order:
1. The words "Commonwealth of Pennsylvania"
2. The words "Notary Seal"
3. The notary public's name (same as on the notary public commission, with the words "Notary Public")
4. Name of county in which the notary maintains an office
5. Date the notary commission expires
6. Notary commission number

An optional embosser may be used in addition (not as a replacement) of the rubber stamp seal.

The rubber stamp seal must be stamped in a prominent place on the notarial certificate.

Journal

The notary public journal (notary register) is used to record all notarial acts (in chronological order) that the notary performs.

Journal may be in a tangible medium or electronic form.

Separate journals for tangible records and electronic records may be maintained.

Paper journals must be bound and have numbered pages.

Electronic journal must comply with the regulations of the Department.

Journal entries must be made contemporaneously with performance of the notarial act. They must include:
1. Date and time of notarial act.
2. Description of record, if any, and type of notarial act.
3. Full name and address (city and state) of each individual for whom the notarial act is performed.
4. Whether identity of individual is based on personal knowledge.
5. Whether identity of individual is based on satisfactory evidence, and if so, brief description of the method of identification and any ID documents presented (with date of issuance and expiration of ID).
6. Fee charged by the notary.

Journal may <u>not</u> contain personal financial or ID information of client, such as full name and full social security number, credit card number or driver's license number.

Certified Copies of Notary Public Journal Pages

1. Notary public must allow inspection of his journal by a person requesting it.
2. To prove that a notarial act took place, the notary can supply a certified copy of journal page. Certification of the notary, attached to the copy of the entire journal page, should read: "I certify that this is a true and correct copy from my official journal in my possession."
3. Notary must provide the certified copy within 10 days of receipt of request.
4. Reasonable copying and postage fees may be charged.
5. A request for inspection of the journal by a law enforcement agency should be complied with in the same manner as a subpoena would be complied with.

ACE THE PENNSYLVANIA NOTARY PUBLIC EXAM

Notary public laws and regulations begin on the following page. Before you start reading the law, here are 4 examples of multiple-choice questions:

1. If a notary changes his office address within the Commonwealth, he must give notice within 5 days to:
A. the Secretary of the Commonwealth only.
B. the Recorder of Deeds of county of original appointment
C. the Recorder of Deeds of county of the new residence
D. the Secretary of the Commonwealth and the Recorder of Deeds of county of original appointment.
Answer: D (Notary Public Law: Section 7)

2. If a notary does not reside or work in the Commonwealth, his commission is deemed resigned and he shall notify in writing _____ of the effective date of the resignation.
A. the recorder of deeds in the county where he did business
B. the prothonotary of the county where he did business or resided
C. the Secretary of the Commonwealth
D. the Comptroller of the Commonwealth
Answer: C (Notary Public Law: Section 7)

3. A notary bond in the amount of $10,000 shall be filed with:
A. the clerk of the county.
B. the Secretary of the Commonwealth.
C. the recorder of deeds in the county where the notary does business.
D. the prothonotary of the county where notary resides.
Answer: B (Notary Public Law: Section 8)

4. In case of death, resignation or disqualification of notary the notary's register and seal must be delivered to _____ within thirty (30) days of the event.
A. office of recorder of deeds of the proper county
B. the Secretary of the Commonwealth
C. the clerk of the county
D. the Commonwealth Comptroller
Answer: A (Notary Public Law: Section 8)

Notes on Reading the Law

The following pages contain:
1. <u>On the left side</u>: notary public **LAW** (edited for format).
2. <u>On the right side</u>: notary public **HIGHLIGHTS** (edited for ease of study).

LAW	**HIGHLIGHTS**

Please note that the unofficial sections of laws and accompanying "highlights" are <u>edited</u> and are presented solely for the purpose of quick study aids and <u>not</u> as legal reference. The primary sources of legal reference are the laws themselves which are available in many places, including online at:

http://www.dos.pa.gov/OtherServices/Notaries/Resources/Pages/Laws-.aspx

---

"Each and every Notary Public plays a crucial role in combating identity theft. They serve as our front line of defense and the public is safer because of the job they do."

- Ken Salazar

LAW

The Notary Public Law (Act No. 373 of 1953, as amended by Act 151 of 2002, effective July 1, 2003)

Section1. Short Title. This act shall be known and may be cited as "The Notary Public Law."

Section 2. Appointment of Notaries. The Secretary of the Commonwealth is hereby authorized to appoint and commission, for a term of four years from the date of appointment, as many notaries public as, in the Secretary's judgment, the interest of the public may require, whose jurisdiction shall be coextensive with the boundaries of the Commonwealth.

Section 3. Eligibility.

(a) Any person who is eighteen (18) years of age or over, who resides or is employed within this Commonwealth and who is of good character, integrity and ability shall be eligible for the office of notary public.

(b) Any person who is a notary public and who resides outside this Commonwealth shall be deemed to have irrevocably appointed the Secretary of the Commonwealth as the person's agent upon whom may be served any summons, subpoena, order or other process.

Section 4. Disqualification; Exception. The following persons shall be ineligible to hold the office of notary public:

(1) Any person holding any judicial office in this Commonwealth, except the office of justice of the peace, magistrate, or alderman.

(2) Every member of Congress, and any person, whether an officer, a subordinate officer, or agent, holding any office or appointment of profit or trust under the legislative, executive, or judiciary departments of the government of

HIGHLIGHTS

The Notary Public Law

Section1. This law shall be known and cited as "**The Notary Public Law**."

Section 2. Appointment of Notaries. The Secretary is authorized to appoint and commission, for a term of 4 years from the date of appointment, notaries whose authority shall be inside the Commonwealth.

Section 3. Eligibility
 (a) A person 18 or over, who resides or is employed in the Commonwealth and is of good character, integrity and ability is eligible to become a notary.

 (b) A person who is a notary and resides outside the Commonwealth is deemed to have irrevocably appointed the Secretary as his agent on whom may be served any summons, subpoena, order or other process.

Section 4. Disqualification; Exception. The following are not eligible to hold the office of notary:
 (1) A person holding any judicial office in Commonwealth, except office of justice of the peace, magistrate, or alderman.

 (2) Every member of Congress, and any officer, a subordinate officer, or agent, holding any office or appointment of profit or trust under the legislative, executive, or judiciary departments of the government of

ACE THE PENNSYLVANIA NOTARY PUBLIC EXAM

LAW

the United States, to which a salary, fees or perquisites are attached.

Section 5. Application to Become a Notary Public.
 (a) Applications for appointment to the office of notary public shall be made to the Secretary of the Commonwealth, on forms prescribed and furnished by the secretary, and shall be accompanied by a nonrefundable filing fee as set forth in section 618-A of the act of April 9, 1929 (P.L. 177, No. 175), known as "The Administrative Code of 1929," payable to the order of the "Commonwealth of Pennsylvania."
Each application shall bear the endorsement of the Senator of the district in which the applicant resides or, if the applicant does not reside in this Commonwealth, the endorsement of the Senator of the district in which the applicant is employed. In the case of a vacancy in that senatorial district, the application shall be endorsed by the Senator of an adjacent district.
 (b) Before issuing to any applicant a commission as notary public, the Secretary of the Commonwealth shall be satisfied that the applicant is of good moral character, and is familiar with the duties and responsibilities of a notary public. The application must contain no material misstatement or omission of fact, and the applicant shall not:
 (1) have been convicted of or pled guilty or nolo contendere to a felony or a lesser offense incompatible with the duties of a notary public during the five (5) year period preceding the date of the application; or
 (2) have had a prior notary public commission revoked by the Commonwealth or any other state during the five (5) year period preceding the date of the application.
The Secretary of the Commonwealth may, for good cause, reject any application of any notary public subject to the right of notice, hearing and adjudication and the right of

ACE THE PENNSYLVANIA NOTARY PUBLIC EXAM

HIGHLIGHTS

the US, to which salary, fees or perks are attached.

Section 5. Application to Become a Notary
(a) Applications for notary public shall be made to Secretary of the Commonwealth, on forms furnished by the Secretary, and shall be accompanied by a nonrefundable filing fee payable to "Commonwealth of Pennsylvania."

(Paragraph Repealed)

(b) Before issuing a notary public commission, the Secretary must be satisfied that applicant is of good moral character and is familiar with the duties and responsibilities of a notary. The application must contain no material misstatement or omission of fact, and applicant shall not:

(1) have been convicted or pled guilty or "no contest" to a felony or a lesser offense incompatible with duties of a notary during the five (5) year period preceding date of application; or
(2) have had a prior notary commission revoked by the Commonwealth or any other state during the five (5) year period preceding date of the application.
The Secretary may, for good cause, reject any notary application subject to the right of notice, hearing and adjudication and the right of

LAW

appeal therefrom in accordance with 2 Pa.C.S. Chs. 5 Subch. A (relating to practice and procedure of Commonwealth agencies) and 7 Subch. A (relating to judicial review of Commonwealth agency action), known as the Administrative Agency Law.

(c) As a condition for the Secretary of the Commonwealth's issuance of a notary commission to an applicant not appointed to the office of notary public as of the effective date of this subsection, a notary applicant must complete at least three (3) hours of approved notary education within the six (6) month period immediately preceding their application.

(d) Notary education may either be interactive or classroom instruction. All education programs shall be preapproved by the Secretary of the Commonwealth with a core curriculum that includes the duties and responsibilities of the notary office and electronic notarization.
Compiler's Note: Section 15 of Act 67 of 1990 provided that section 5 is repealed insofar as it relates to fee payments.

Section 6. Application for Reappointment. Applications for reappointment to the office of notary public shall be filed at least two months prior to the expiration of the commission under which the notary is acting. Persons seeking reappointment must continue to meet the requirements set forth in section 5 in order to be reappointed.

Section 7. Vacation of Office; Change of Residence.
(a) In the event of any change of address within the Commonwealth, notice in writing or electronically shall be given to the Secretary of the Commonwealth and the

HIGHLIGHTS

appeal according to 2 Pa.C.S. Chs. 5 Subch. A (Practice and procedure of Commonwealth agencies) and 7 Subch. A (Judicial review of Commonwealth agency action), known as the Administrative Agency Law.

(c) For the Secretary to issue a notary commission, applicant must complete at least (3) hours of approved notary education within the (6) month period preceding the application.

(d) Notary education may be interactive or classroom instruction. All education programs shall be preapproved by the Secretary with a core curriculum that includes the duties and responsibilities of the notary office and electronic notarization.

Section 6. Application for Reappointment

Applications for reappointment shall be filed at least (2) months prior to expiration of commission.
Persons seeking reappointment must continue to meet requirements in section 5 in order to be reappointed.

Section 7. Vacation of Office; Change of Residence

(a) If the notary changes address within the Commonwealth, notice in writing or electronically shall be given to the Secretary and the

LAW

recorder of deeds of the county of original appointment by a notary public within five (5) days of such change. For the purpose of this subsection, "address" means office address. A notary public vacates his office by removing the notary's residence and business address from the Commonwealth, and such removal shall constitute a resignation from the office of notary public as of the date of removal.

(b) If a notary public neither resides nor works in the Commonwealth, that notary public shall be deemed to have resigned from the office of notary public as of the date the residency ceases or employment within the Commonwealth terminates. A notary public who resigns that notary's commission in accordance with this subsection shall notify the Secretary of the Commonwealth in writing of the effective date of the resignation.

Section 8. Oath of Office; Bond; Recording.
Every notary, upon appointment and prior to entering upon the duties of the office of notary public, shall take and subscribe the constitutional oath of office, and shall give a surety bond, payable to the Commonwealth of Pennsylvania, in the amount of ten thousand dollars ($ 10,000), which bond shall, after being recorded, be approved by and filed with the Secretary of the Commonwealth. Every such bond shall have as surety a duly authorized surety company or two sufficient individual sureties, to be approved by the Secretary of the Commonwealth, conditioned for the faithful performance of the duties of the office of notary public and for the delivery of the notary's register and seal to the office of the recorder of deeds of the proper county in case of the death, resignation or disqualification of the notary within thirty (30) days of such event.

HIGHLIGHTS

recorder of deeds of county of original appointment within five (5) days of change. "Address" means office address. If a notary vacates his office by removing notary's residence and business address from the Commonwealth, removal shall constitute a resignation from office of notary as of the date of removal.

(b) If a notary does not reside or work in Commonwealth, notary shall be deemed to have resigned from the office of notary as of the date the residency ceases or employment within Commonwealth terminates. A notary who resigns his commission in accordance with this subsection shall notify the Secretary in writing of the effective date of resignation.

Section 8. Oath of Office; Bond; Recording
Every notary, upon appointment and prior to entering the duties of notary, shall take and subscribe the constitutional oath of office, and shall give a surety bond, payable to the Commonwealth of Pennsylvania, in the amount of ten thousand dollars ($ 10,000), which shall, after being recorded, be approved by and filed with the Secretary. Every bond shall have as surety a duly authorized surety company **or** 2 sufficient individual sureties, to be approved by the Secretary, conditioned for the faithful performance of the duties of the notary and for delivery of notary's register and seal to office of recorder of deeds of the proper county in case of death, resignation or disqualification of notary within thirty (30) days of the event.

LAW

Such bond, as well as the commission and oath of office, shall be recorded in the office of the recorder of deeds of the county in which the notary maintains an office at the time of appointment or reappointment. The commission of any notary hereafter appointed who shall, for forty-five (45) days after the beginning of the term, neglect to give bond and cause the bond and the commission and oath to be recorded, as above directed, shall be null and void.

Section 9. Registration of Notary's Signature; Fee.
(a) The official signature of each notary public shall be registered, in the "Notary Register" provided for such purpose in the prothonotary's office of the county wherein the notary maintains an office, within forty-five (45) days after appointment or reappointment, and in any county to which the notary may subsequently move the notary's office, within thirty (30) days thereafter. In counties of the second class, such signature shall also be registered in the clerk of courts' office within said period.
(b) The fee to be charged by the prothonotary for recording a notary's signature shall be fifty ($ .50) cents.
(c) In acting as a notary public, a notary shall sign the notary's name exactly and only as it appears on the commission or otherwise execute the notary's electronic signature in a manner that attributes such signature to the notary public identified on the commission.
(d) A county may permit notaries to register their electronic signatures.

Section 10. Change of Name. Whenever the name of any notary is changed by decree of court, or otherwise, such notary may continue to perform official acts, in the name in which he or she was commissioned, until the expiration of his or her term, but he or she shall, within thirty (30) days after entry of such decree, or after such name change, if not by decree of court, notify the Secretary of the

HIGHLIGHTS

Bond, commission and oath of office, shall be recorded in office of the recorder of deeds of county in which notary maintains an office at time of appointment or reappointment. If notary neglects to give the bond, and record the bond, commission and oath within forty-five (45) days after beginning of his term, commission shall be null and void.

Section 9. Registration of Notary's Signature; Fee
(a) Official signature of notary shall be registered, in the "Notary Register" in the prothonotary's office of county where notary maintains an office, within (45) days after appointment or reappointment, and in any county to which notary may subsequently move the notary's office, within (30) days thereafter. In counties of the second class, such signature shall also be registered in the clerk of courts' office within said period.
(b) Fee to be charged by prothonotary for recording a notary's signature is fifty ($ .50) cents.
(c) In acting as a notary, a notary shall sign the notary's name exactly as it appears on the commission or otherwise execute notary's electronic signature in a manner that attributes such signature to the notary public identified on the commission.
(d) A county may permit notaries to register their electronic signatures.

Section 10. Change of Name. When the name of a notary is changed by court decree, or otherwise, notary may continue to perform official acts, in the name in which he was commissioned, until expiration of his term, but must, within thirty (30) days after entry of such decree, or after such name change, if not by decree of court, notify the Secretary of the

LAW

Commonwealth and recorder of deeds of the county in which he or she maintains an office of such change of name. The Secretary of the Commonwealth shall mark the public records relating to the notary accordingly and recorder of deeds shall record the notification. Application for reappointment of such notary shall be made in the new name.

Section 11. Refund of Fee. (Repealed June 30, 1988, P.L. 462, No. 78)

Section 12. Notarial Seal.
 (a) A notary public shall provide and keep an official seal which shall be used to authenticate all the acts, instruments and attestations of the notary. The seal shall be a rubber stamp and shall show clearly in the following order: the words "Notarial Seal"; the name and surname of the notary and the words "Notary Public"; the name of the municipality and county in which the notary maintains an office; and the date the notary's commission expires.
 (b) The seal shall have a maximum height of one (1) inch and width of three and one-half (3 1/2) inches, with a plain border. It shall be stamped in a prominent place on the official notarial certificate near the notary's signature in such a manner as to be capable of photographic reproduction.
 (c) (Deleted by Act 151 of 2002, effective July 1, 2003)
 (d) The notary public seal is the exclusive property of the notary to whom it is issued, and a notary shall be responsible at all times for maintaining custody and control of the seal. No notary public shall permit the use of the seal by another person.
 (e) The use of a notary public seal by a person who is not the notary public named on the seal shall be deemed an impersonation of a notary public under and shall be subject

HIGHLIGHTS

Commonwealth and the recorder of deeds of county where he maintains an office of such change of name. Secretary shall mark the public records accordingly and the recorder of deeds shall record the notification. Application for reappointment of such notary shall be made in the <u>new</u> name.

Section 11. Refund of Fee. (Repealed June 30, 1988)

Section 12. Notarial Seal

(a) Notary shall provide and keep an official seal used to authenticate acts, instruments and attestations. Seal shall be a <u>rubber stamp</u> and show clearly in following order: the words <u>"Notarial Seal"; the name and surname of the notary and the words "Notary Public"; the name of the</u> ~~municipality~~ <u>(repealed) and county in which the notary maintains an office; and the date the notary's commission expires</u>.

(b) Seal shall have a maximum height of one (1) inch and width of three and one-half (3 1/2) inches, with a plain border.
<u>Seal shall be stamped in a prominent place on official notarial certificate near notary's signature in a manner as to be capable of photographic reproduction.</u>

(c) (Deleted by Act 151 of 2002, effective July 1, 2003)

(d) <u>Notary seal is exclusive property of notary to whom</u> it is issued, and a notary shall be responsible at all times for maintaining custody and control of the seal.
<u>No notary public shall permit use of the seal by another person.</u>

(e) The use of a notary seal by a person who is not the notary named on the seal shall be deemed an impersonation of a notary and shall be subject

LAW

to the penalties set forth in 18 Pa.C.S. § 4913 (relating to impersonating a notary public).
 (f) Notwithstanding other provisions of this section, in accordance with the act of December 16, 1999
(P.L. 971, No. 69), known as the "Electronic Transactions Act," a notary public is not required to use an electronic seal for the notarization, acknowledgment or verification of electronic records and electronic signatures, provided that, in any event, the following information is attached to or logically associated with the electronic signature or electronic record being notarized, acknowledged or verified:
 (1) The full name of the notary along with the words "Notary Public."
 (2) The name of the municipality and the county in which the notary maintains an office.
 (3) The date the notary's commission is due to expire.

 (a) The officer notarizing the instrument shall know through personal knowledge or have satisfactory evidence that the person appearing before the notary is the person described in and who is executing the instrument. For the purposes of this act and section 5 of the act of July 24, 1941 (P.L.490, No.188), known as the "Uniform Acknowledgment Act," "personal knowledge" means having an acquaintance, derived from association with the individual in relation to other people and based upon a chain of circumstances surrounding the individual, which establishes the individual's identity, and "satisfactory evidence" means the reliance on the presentation of a current, government-issued identification card bearing a photograph, signature or physical description and serial or identification number, or the oath or affirmation of a credible witness who is personally known to the notary and who personally knows the individual.

HIGHLIGHTS

to penalties in 18 Pa.C.S. § 4913 (impersonating a notary public).

(f) Regardless of the other provisions of this section, a notary is **not** required to use an electronic seal for notarization, acknowledgment or verification of electronic records and electronic signatures, provided that the following information is attached to or logically associated with electronic signature or electronic record being notarized, acknowledged or verified:

(1) Full name of the notary, and Notary Public."
(2) County where notary maintains an office.
(3) Date notary's commission is due to expire.

(a) Officer notarizing instrument must know through **personal knowledge** or have **satisfactory evidence** that person appearing before him is person described in and who is executing the instrument.

"**Personal knowledge**" means having an acquaintance, derived from association with individual in relation to other people and based on circumstances surrounding the individual, which establishes the individual's identity.

"**Satisfactory evidence**" means reliance on the presentation of a current, government-issued identification card bearing a photograph, signature or physical description and serial or identification number, or oath or affirmation of a credible witness who is personally known to the notary and who personally knows the individual.

LAW

(b) In certifying a copy of a document or other item, a notary public shall determine that the proffered copy is a full, true and accurate transcription or reproduction of that which was copied.

Section 13. Date of Expiration of Commission. (Repealed June 30, 1988, P.L. 462, No. 78)

Section 14. Position of Seal and Date of Expiration of Commission. – (Repealed June 30, 1988, P.L. 462, No. 78)

Section 15. Register; Copies of Records.
 (a) Every notary public shall keep and maintain custody and control of an accurate chronological register of all official acts by that notary done by virtue of that notary's office, and shall, when thereunto required, give a certified copy of the register in the notary's office to any person applying for same. Each register shall contain the date of the act, the character of the act, and the date and parties to the instrument, and the amount of fee collected for the service. Each notarization shall be indicated separately.
 (b) The register and other public records of such notary shall not in any case be liable to be seized, attached or taken in execution for debt or for any demand whatsoever.
 (c) A notary public register is the exclusive property of the notary public, may not be used by any other person and may not be surrendered to any employer of the notary upon termination of employment.
 (d) Upon a notary public's resignation, death or disqualification or upon the revocation or expiration of a commission, unless the notary public applies for a commission within thirty (30) days of the expiration of the prior commission, the notary public's register shall be delivered to the office of the recorder of deeds of the proper county within thirty (30) days of such event.

HIGHLIGHTS

(b) When certifying a copy of a document or other item, a notary must determine that copy is a full, true and accurate transcription or reproduction of what was copied.

Section 13. Date of Expiration of Commission. (Repealed June 30, 1988, P.L. 462, No. 78)

Section 14. Position of Seal and Date of Expiration of Commission. – (Repealed June 30, 1988, P.L. 462, No. 78)

Section 15. Register; Copies of Records

(a) Every notary shall keep and maintain custody and control of an accurate chronological register of all official acts by notary done, and shall, when required, give a certified copy of register in notary's office to any person applying for it.
Each register shall contain date of act, character of act, and date and parties to the instrument, and amount of fee collected for service. Each notarization shall be indicated separately.

(b) Register and other public records of notary shall not be liable to be seized, attached or taken in execution for debt or for any demand.

(c) A notary public register is exclusive property of notary, may not be used by any other person and may not be surrendered to any employer of notary upon termination of employment.

(d) Upon a notary's resignation, death or disqualification or upon revocation or expiration of a commission, unless notary applies for a commission within thirty (30) days of expiration of prior commission, notary's register shall be delivered to the office of the recorder of deeds of the proper county within thirty (30) days of such event.

LAW

Section 16. Power to Administer Oaths and Affirmations.
 (a) Notaries shall have power to administer oaths and affirmations, certify copies and take depositions, affidavits, verifications, upon oath or affirmation and acknowledgments according to law, in all matters belonging or incident to the exercise of their notarial office.
 (b) Any person who shall be convicted of having willfully and knowingly made or taken a false oath, affirmation, deposition, affidavit, certification or acknowledgment before any notary in any matters within their official duties shall be guilty of perjury under and shall be subject to the penalties set forth in 18 Pa.C.S. § 4902 (relating to perjury).

Section 17. Power to take Acknowledgment of Instruments of Writing Relating to Commerce or Navigation and to Make Declarations. Repealed by 2002, Dec. 9, P.L. 1269, No. 151, effective July 1, 2003

Section 18. Power to Take Depositions, Affidavits and Acknowledgment of Writings Relative to Lands. Repealed by 2002, Dec. 9, P.L. 1269, No. 151, effective July 1, 2003

Section 19. Limitation on Powers; Fees.
 (a) to (c) (Deleted by Act 151 of 2002, effective July 1, 2003.)
 (d) No district justice, holding at the same time the office of notary public, shall have jurisdiction in cases arising on papers or documents containing acts by him done in the office of notary public.
 (e) No notary public may act as such in any transaction in which he is a party directly or pecuniarily interested. For the purpose of this section, none of the following shall constitute a direct or pecuniary interest:

HIGHLIGHTS

Section 16. Power to Administer Oaths and Affirmations

(a) Notaries have power to <u>administer oaths and affirmations, certify copies and take depositions, affidavits, verifications, upon oath or affirmation and acknowledgments</u>, in all matters in their exercise of their notarial office.

(b) Any person convicted of having willfully and knowingly made or taken a false oath, affirmation, deposition, affidavit, certification or acknowledgment before a notary is guilty of <u>perjury</u> and subject to penalties in 18 Pa.C.S. § 4902 (relating to perjury).

Section 17. Power to take Acknowledgment of Instruments of Writing Relating to Commerce or Navigation and to Make Declarations. Repealed by 2002, Dec. 9, P.L. 1269, No. 151, effective July 1, 2003

Section 18. Power to Take Depositions, Affidavits and Acknowledgment of Writings Relative to Lands. Repealed by 2002, Dec. 9, P.L. 1269, No. 151, effective July 1, 2003

Section 19. Limitation on Powers; Fees
(a) to (c) (Deleted by Act 151 of 2002, effective 7/1/2003.)

(d) No district justice, who is a notary, has jurisdiction in cases arising on papers or documents containing acts by him done in the office of notary.

(e) <u>No notary may act as such in any transaction in which he is a party directly or pecuniarily (involving money) interested</u>. For purpose of this section, <u>none</u> of following is a direct or pecuniary interest:

LAW

(1) being a shareholder in a publicly traded company that is a party to the notarized transaction;
(2) being an officer, director or employee of a company that is a party to the notarized transaction, unless the director, officer or employee personally benefits from the transaction other than as provided in clause (3); or
(3) receiving a fee that is not contingent upon the completion of the notarized transaction.

Section 20. Admissibility in Evidence. Repealed April 28, 1978, P.L. 202, No. 53, effective June 27, 1978

Section 21. Fees of Notaries Public.
(a) The fees of notaries public shall be fixed by the Secretary of the Commonwealth with the approval of the Attorney General.
(b) A notary public shall not charge, attempt to charge or receive a notary public fee that is in excess of the fees fixed by the Secretary of the Commonwealth.
(c) The fees of notaries public shall be displayed in a conspicuous location in the notary's place of business or be provided upon request to any person utilizing the services of the notary. The fees of the notary shall be separately stated. A notary public may waive the right to charge a fee, in which case the requirements of this subsection regarding the display or provision of fees shall not apply.
(d) The fee for any notary public employed by a bank, banking institution or trust company shall be the property of the notary and in no case belong to or be received by the corporation for whom the notary is employed.

Section 22. Rejection of Application; Removal. (a) The Secretary of the Commonwealth may, for good cause, reject any application, issue a written reprimand, suspend or revoke the commission of any notary public.

HIGHLIGHTS

(1) being a shareholder in a publicly traded company that is a party to notarized transaction;
(2) being an officer, director or employee of a company that is a party to notarized transaction, unless director, officer or employee personally benefits from transaction other than as provided in clause (3); or
(3) receiving a fee not contingent on completion of notarized transaction.

Section 20. Admissibility in Evidence. Repealed April 28, 1978, P.L. 202, No. 53, effective June 27, 1978

Section 21. Fees of Notaries Public.
(a) <u>Fees of notaries are fixed by Secretary of the Commonwealth with approval of the Attorney General.</u>

(b) Notary shall not charge, attempt to charge or receive a notary fee <u>greater</u> than fees fixed by Secretary.

(c) Fees of notaries shall be displayed in a conspicuous location in notary's place of business or be provided on request to any person utilizing services of notary. Fees of notary shall be separately stated. <u>Notary may waive right to charge a fee</u> (in which case requirements of this subsection on display or provision of fees do <u>not</u> apply).

(d) <u>Fee for a notary employed by a bank, banking institution or trust company shall be property of notary and in no case belong to or be received by the corporation for whom notary is employed</u>.

Section 22. Rejection of Application; Removal
(a) Secretary may reject any application, issue a written reprimand, suspend or revoke commission of a notary.

LAW

(1) (b) The Secretary of the Commonwealth may, for good cause, impose a civil penalty not to exceed five hundred dollars ($ 500) for each act or omission which constitutes a violation of this act.
(c) The Secretary of the Commonwealth may, for good cause, order a notary to attend education courses for an act or omission which constitutes a violation of this act.
(d) Any action taken under this section shall be subject to the right of notice, hearing and adjudication,
and the right of appeal therefrom, in accordance with 2 Pa.C.S. Chs. 5 Subch. A (relating to practice and procedure of Commonwealth agencies) and 7 Subch. A (relating to judicial review of Commonwealth
agency action), known as the Administrative Agency Law.

Section 22.1. Surrender of Seal.
(a) Should an application or renewal be rejected, or should a commission be revoked or recalled for any
reason, or should a notary public resign, the applicant or notary shall deliver the seal of office to the Department of State within ten (10) days after notice from the department or from the date of resignation, as the case may be. Any person who violates the provisions of this subsection shall be guilty of a summary offense and upon conviction thereof shall be sentenced to pay a fine not exceeding three hundred dollars ($ 300) or to imprisonment not exceeding ninety (90) days, or both.
(b) Upon the death of a notary public, the notary's personal representative shall deliver the seal of office to the Department of State within ninety (90) days of the date of the notary's death.

Section 22.2. Revocation of Commission for Certain Personal Checks.
(a) The Secretary of the Commonwealth may revoke the notary public commission of a notary public who issues to

HIGHLIGHTS

(b) Secretary may impose a civil penalty <u>not to exceed five hundred dollars ($ 500)</u> for each act or omission which constitutes a violation of this act.

(c) Secretary may order a notary to attend education courses for an act or omission which constitutes a violation of this act.

(d) Any action taken under this section shall be subject to right of notice, hearing and adjudication, and right of appeal, in accordance with 2 Pa.C.S. Chs. 5 Subch. A (relating to practice and procedure of Commonwealth agencies) and 7 Subch. A (relating to judicial review of Commonwealth agency action), known as the Administrative Agency Law.

Section 22.1. Surrender of Seal

(a) If an application or renewal is rejected, or a commission is revoked or recalled, or if a notary resigns, applicant or notary shall deliver seal of office to Department of State within <u>ten (10) days after notice from department or from date of resignation</u>.
Any person who violates provisions of this subsection shall be guilty of a <u>summary offense</u> and on conviction shall be sentenced to pay a <u>fine not more than $300 hundred dollars or imprisonment not more than 90 days, or both.</u>

(b) Upon death of a notary, notary's personal representative shall deliver the seal of office to Department of State <u>within 90 days of date of notary's death</u>.

Section 22.2. Revocation of Commission for Certain Personal Checks

(a) Secretary may revoke commission of a notary who issues to

ACE THE PENNSYLVANIA NOTARY PUBLIC EXAM

LAW

the order of any State agency or the Commonwealth a personal check without sufficient funds on deposit.

(b) Any action taken by the Secretary of the Commonwealth under this section shall be subject to the right of notice, hearing and adjudication and right of appeal therefrom in accordance with 2 Pa.C.S. Chs. 5 Subch. A relating to practice and procedure of Commonwealth agencies) and 7 Subch. A (relating to judicial review of Commonwealth agency action), known as the Administrative Agency Law.

Section 22.3. Regulations. The Secretary of the Commonwealth shall have the authority to promulgate such rules and regulations as are necessary to administer and enforce this act.

Section 23. Specific Repeal. The act, approved the eighteenth day of May, one thousand nine hundred forty-nine (Pamphlet Laws 1440), entitled "An act concerning notaries public and amending, revising, consolidating and changing the law relating thereto," is hereby repealed absolutely.

Section 24. Repeals. (a) The following acts and parts of acts are repealed:
The act of April 14, 1828 (P.L.447, No.188), entitled "An act to authorizes the appointment of commissioners to take the acknowledgement of deeds and instruments of writing under seal."
The act of March 13, 1839 (P.L.92, No.44), entitled "A supplement to an act entitled 'An act to authorize the appointment of commissioners to take the acknowledgment of deeds and instruments of writing under seal,' approved on the fourteenth day of April, one thousand eight hundred and twenty- eight."
The act of April 6, 1843 (P.L.175, No.83), entitled "A supplement to an act entitled 'An Act to authorize the appointment of Commissioners to take the acknowledgment of deeds and instruments of writing under seal.'" Section 15 of the act of April 9, 1849 (P.L.524, No.354), entitled "A supplement to an act relative to the venders of mineral waters; and an act relative to the Washington coal company; to sheriffs' sales of real estate; to the substitution of executors and trustees when plaintiffs; to partition in the courts of common pleas, and for other purposes."
(b) All other acts and parts of acts are repealed insofar as they are inconsistent with this act.

HIGHLIGHTS

the order of any State agency or Commonwealth a personal check without <u>sufficient funds</u> on deposit.

(b) Any action taken by Secretary under this section is subject to right of notice, hearing, adjudication and appeal in accordance with 2 Pa.C.S. Chs. 5 Subch. A, relating to practice and procedure of Commonwealth agencies) and 7 Subch. A (relating to judicial review of Commonwealth agency action), known as the Administrative Agency Law.

Section 22.3. Regulations. The Secretary has the authority to promulgate rules and regulations to administer and enforce this act.

Section 23. Specific Repeal. The act, approved the eighteenth day of May, one thousand nine hundred forty-nine (Pamphlet Laws 1440), entitled "An act concerning notaries public and amending, revising, consolidating and changing the law relating thereto," is hereby repealed absolutely.

Section 24. Repeals. (a) The following acts and parts of acts are repealed:
The act of April 14, 1828 (P.L.447, No.188), entitled "An act to authorizes the appointment of commissioners to take the acknowledgement of deeds and instruments of writing under seal."
The act of March 13, 1839 (P.L.92, No.44), entitled "A supplement to an act entitled 'An act to authorize the appointment of commissioners to take the acknowledgment of deeds and instruments of writing under seal,' approved on the fourteenth day of April, one thousand eight hundred and twenty- eight."
The act of April 6, 1843 (P.L.175, No.83), entitled "A supplement to an act entitled 'An Act to authorize the appointment of Commissioners to take the acknowledgment of deeds and instruments of writing under seal.'" Section 15 of the act of April 9, 1849 (P.L.524, No.354), entitled "A supplement to an act relative to the venders of mineral waters; and an act relative to the Washington coal company; to sheriffs' sales of real estate; to the substitution of executors and trustees when plaintiffs; to partition in the courts of common pleas, and for other purposes."
(b) All other acts and parts of acts are repealed insofar as they are inconsistent with this act.

LAW

301. Short title of chapter.
This chapter shall be known and may be cited as the Revised Uniform Law on Notarial Acts.

-----

302. Definitions.
The following words and phrases when used in this chapter shall have the meanings given to them in this section unless the context clearly indicates otherwise:

"Acknowledgment." A declaration by an individual before a notarial officer that:

   (1) the individual has signed a record for the purpose stated in the record; and

   (2) if the record is signed in a representative capacity, the individual signed the record with proper authority and signed it as the act of the individual or entity identified in the record.

"Bureau." The Bureau of Commissions, Elections and Legislation.

"Conviction." Whether or not judgment of sentence has been imposed, any of the following:
(1) An entry of a plea of guilty or nolo contendere.
(2) A guilty verdict, whether after trial by judge or by jury.
(3) A finding of not guilty due to insanity or of guilty but mentally ill.

"Department." The Department of State of the Commonwealth.

HIGHLIGHTS

301. This law shall be known as the
"Revised Uniform Law on Notarial Acts" (RULONA).

-----

302 The following are definitions used in this law:

"Acknowledgment" is a declaration made in front of a notary that:
   (1) person signed the record for the reason stated in the record; and that
   (2) if person signed as a representative, he did so with proper authority.

"Bureau" is short for:
"The Bureau of Commissions, Elections and Legislation."

"Conviction" means any of the following, even if a sentence was not ordered by a court:
   (1) An entry of a plea of guilty or "no contest".
   (2) A guilty verdict in a trial (with or without a jury).
   (3) A finding of not guilty due to insanity, or guilty but mentally ill.

"Department" means:
"The Department of State of the Commonwealth"

LAW

"Electronic" Relating to technology having electrical, digital, magnetic, wireless, optical, electromagnetic or similar capabilities.

"Electronic signature." An electronic symbol, sound or process attached to or logically associated with a record and executed or adopted by an individual with the intent to sign the record.

"In a representative capacity." Acting as:
- (1) an authorized officer, agent, partner, trustee or other representative for a person other than an individual;
- (2) a public officer, personal representative, guardian or other representative, in the capacity stated in a record;
- (3) an agent or attorney-in-fact for a principal; or
- (4) an authorized representative of another in any other capacity.

"Notarial act." An act, whether performed with respect to a tangible or electronic record, that a notarial officer may perform under the laws of this Commonwealth. The term includes:
- (1) taking an acknowledgment;
- (2) administering an oath or affirmation;
- (3) taking a verification on oath or affirmation;
- (4) witnessing or attesting a signature;
- (5) certifying or attesting a copy or deposition; and
- (6) noting a protest of a negotiable instrument.

"Notarial officer." A notary public or other individual authorized to perform a notarial act.

HIGHLIGHTS

"Electronic" means having electronic capabilities.

"Electronic signature" is an electronic indication in an electronic record verifying intent to sign the document.

"In a representative capacity" means a person is acting as:
  (1) an authorized officer or representative;
  (2) a public officer, or personal representative in the capacity stated in a record;
  (3) an authorized agent or attorney
  (4) an authorized representative.

"Notarial act" is an act performed by a notarial officer under laws of this Commonwealth. It includes:
  (1) taking an acknowledgment;
  (2) administering an oath or affirmation;
  (3) taking a verification on oath or affirmation;
  (4) witnessing or attesting a signature;
  (5) certifying or attesting a copy or deposition; and
  (6) noting a protest of a negotiable instrument

"Notarial officer" is a notary or other person authorized to perform a notarial act.

LAW

"Notary public." An individual commissioned to perform a notarial act by the department.

"Official stamp." A physical image affixed to or embossed on a tangible record or an electronic image attached to or logically associated with an electronic record. The term includes a notary public seal.

"Person." Any of the following:
    (1) Any individual, corporation, business trust, statutory trust, estate, trust, partnership, limited liability company, association, joint venture or public corporation.
    (2) A government or governmental subdivision, agency or instrumentality.
    (3) Any other legal or commercial entity.

"Record." Information that is inscribed on a tangible medium or that is stored in an electronic or other medium and is retrievable in perceivable form.

"Recorder of deeds." A county recorder of deeds or an official with similar duties and responsibilities. The term includes the commissioner of records of a county of the first class and the manager of the department of real estate of a county of the second class.

"Secretary." The Secretary of the Commonwealth

HIGHLIGHTS

"Notary public" is a person commissioned to perform a notarial act.

"Official stamp" (includes a notary seal) is a physical image <u>attached to or embossed</u> on a tangible record (paper) or an <u>electronic image</u> in an electronic record.

"Person" is:
- (1) Individual, corporation, business trust, statutory trust, estate, trust, partnership, limited liability company, association, joint venture or public corporation.
- (2) Government or governmental subdivision, agency or instrumentality.
- (3) Any other legal or commercial entity.

"Record" is information on a medium (example: paper) or stored in an electronic or other medium.

"Recorder of deeds" is a county recorder of deeds or an official with similar duties, including commissioner of records of a county of the first class and manager of department of real estate of a county of the second class.

"Secretary" means the Secretary of the Commonwealth.

LAW

"Sign" With present intent to authenticate or adopt a record:
    (1) to execute or adopt a tangible symbol; or
    (2) to attach to or logically associate with the record an electronic symbol, sound or process.

"Signature" A tangible symbol or an electronic signature which evidenced the signing of a record.

"Stamping device." Any of the following:
    (1) A physical device capable of affixing to or embossing on a tangible record an official stamp.
    (2) An electronic device or process capable of attaching to or logically associating with an electronic record an official stamp.

"State." A state of the United States, the District of Columbia, Puerto Rico, the Virgin Islands or any territory or insular possession subject to the jurisdiction of the United States.

"Verification on oath or affirmation." A declaration, made by an individual on oath or affirmation before a notarial officer, that a statement in a record is true. The term includes an affidavit.

-----

303. Applicability
This chapter applies to a notarial act performed on or after the effective date of this chapter.

ACE THE PENNSYLVANIA NOTARY PUBLIC EXAM

HIGHLIGHTS

"Sign" with intent to authenticate or adopt a record means:
  (1) to execute or adopt a tangible symbol
      (example: signature); or
  (2) to attach to or include with record an electronic symbol, sound or process (electronic signature).

"Signature" is a tangible symbol (<u>written signature</u>) or <u>electronic signature</u> which shows signing of a record.

"Stamping device" means:
  (1) A physical device able to affix or emboss on a tangible record an official stamp.
  (2) An electronic device or process able of attaching to an electronic record an official stamp.

"State" means a US state, District of Columbia, Puerto Rico, Virgin Islands, or territory or possession of the US.

"Verification on oath or affirmation" is a declaration, made by a person on oath or affirmation before a notarial officer, that a statement in a record is true. The term includes an affidavit.

-----

303. Applicability of this law
This law applies to notarial acts performed on or after October 26, 2017.

LAW

304. Authority to perform notarial act.
   (a) Permitted. A notarial officer may perform a notarial act authorized by this chapter or by statutory provision other than this chapter.
   (b) Prohibited.
       (1) A notarial officer may not perform a notarial act with respect to a record in which the notarial officer or the notarial officer's spouse has a direct or pecuniary interest.
       (2) For the purpose of this subsection, none of the following shall constitute a direct or pecuniary interest:
           (i) being a shareholder in a publicly traded company that is a party to the notarized transaction;
           (ii) being an officer, director or employee of a company that is a party to the notarized transaction, unless the director, officer or employee personally benefits from the transaction other than as provided under subparagraph (iii); or
           (iii) receiving a fee that is not contingent upon the completion of the notarized transaction.
       (3) A notarial act performed in violation of this subsection is voidable.

-----

305. Requirements for certain notarial acts.
   (a) Acknowledgments. A notarial officer who takes an acknowledgment of a record shall determine, from personal knowledge or satisfactory evidence of the identity of the individual, all of the following:
       (1) The individual appearing before the notarial officer and making the acknowledgment has the identity claimed.

HIGHLIGHTS

304. Authority to perform notarial act
(a) **Permitted**. A notarial officer may perform a notarial act authorized by this law or by other statutory provisions.
(b) **Prohibited**.
  (1) Notarial officer may not perform notarial act with respect to a record in which notarial officer or notarial officer's spouse has a direct or pecuniary interest.
  (2) For purpose of this subsection, **none** of following constitutes a direct or pecuniary interest:
    (i) being a shareholder in a publicly traded company that is a party to notarized transaction;
    (ii) being an officer, director or employee of a company that is a party to notarized transaction, unless director, officer or employee personally benefits from transaction other than as provided under subparagraph (iii); or
    (iii) receiving a fee not contingent on completion of notarized transaction.

  (3) Notarial act performed in violation of this subsection is voidable.

-----

305. Requirements for certain notarial acts
(a) **Acknowledgments:** Notarial officer who takes an acknowledgment of a record shall determine, from personal knowledge or satisfactory evidence of identity of the person, all of following:
  (1) Person appearing before notarial officer and making acknowledgment is person claimed.

LAW

      (2) The signature on the record is the signature of the individual.
 (b) **Verifications**. A notarial officer who takes a verification of a statement on oath or affirmation shall determine, from personal knowledge or satisfactory evidence of the identity of the individual, all of the following:
      (1) The individual appearing before the notarial officer and making the verification has the identity claimed.
      (2) The signature on the statement verified is the signature of the individual.
 (c) **Signatures**. A notarial officer who witnesses or attests to a signature shall determine, from personal knowledge or satisfactory evidence of the identity of the individual, all of the following:
      (1) The individual appearing before the notarial officer and signing the record has the identity claimed.
      (2) The signature on the record is the signature of the individual.
 (d) **Copies**. A notarial officer who certifies or attests a copy of a record or an item which was copied shall determine that the copy is a complete and accurate transcription or reproduction of the record or item.
 (e) **Negotiable instruments.** A notarial officer who makes or notes a protest of a negotiable instrument shall determine the matters set forth in 13 Pa.C.S. § 3505(b) (relating to evidence of dishonor)

-----

306. Personal appearance required.
If a notarial act relates to a statement made in or a signature executed on a record, the individual making the statement or executing the signature shall appear personally before the notarial officer.

HIGHLIGHTS

(2) Signature on record is signature of person.

(b) **Verifications**: Notarial officer who takes a verification of a statement on oath or affirmation shall determine, from <u>personal knowledge or satisfactory evidence of identity of person</u>, all of following:
   (1) Person appearing before notarial officer and making verification is person claimed.
   (2) Signature on statement verified is signature of person.

(c) **Signatures:** Notarial officer who witnesses or attests to a signature shall determine, <u>from personal knowledge or satisfactory evidence of identity of person</u>, all of following:
   (1) Person appearing before notarial officer and signing record is person claimed.
   (2) Signature on record is signature of person.

(d) **Copies**: Notarial officer who certifies or attests a copy of a record or an item which was copied shall determine that copy is a complete and accurate transcription or reproduction of record or item.

(e) **Negotiable instruments:** Notarial officer who makes or notes a protest of a negotiable instrument shall determine matters set forth in 13 Pa.C.S. § 3505(b) (relating to evidence of dishonor)

-----

306. Personal appearance is required
If a notarial act relates to a statement made in or a signature executed on a record, person making statement or executing signature <u>shall appear personally</u> before the notary.

LAW

307. Identification of individual.
   (a) Personal knowledge. A notarial officer has personal knowledge of the identity of an individual appearing before the notarial officer if the individual is personally known to the notarial officer through dealings sufficient to provide reasonable certainty that the individual has the identity claimed.
   (b) Satisfactory evidence. A notarial officer has satisfactory evidence of the identity of an individual appearing before the notarial officer if the notarial officer can identify the individual as set forth in any of the following paragraphs:
      (1) By means set forth in any of the following subparagraphs:
         (i) A passport, driver's license or government-issued nondriver identification card, which is current and unexpired.
         (ii) Another form of government identification issued to an individual, which:
            (A) is current;
            (B) contains the signature or a photograph of the individual; and
            (C) is satisfactory to the notarial officer.
      (2) By a verification on oath or affirmation of a credible witness personally appearing before the notarial officer and personally known to the notarial officer.
   (c) Discretion. A notarial officer may require an individual to provide additional information or identification credentials necessary to assure the notarial officer of the identity of the individual.

HIGHLIGHTS

307. Identification of individual

(a) **Personal knowledge**: Notarial officer has personal knowledge of identity of a person appearing before him if person is known to notarial officer through dealings sufficient to provide reasonable certainty that individual is person claimed.

(b) **Satisfactory evidence**: Notarial officer has satisfactory evidence of identity of a person appearing before him if notarial officer can identify person as follows:
  (1) By means set forth in any of following subparagraphs:
    (i) A passport, driver's license or government-issued nondriver identification card (current and unexpired).
    (ii) Another form of government identification issued to an individual, which:
      (A) is current;
      (B) contains signature or a photograph of individual; and
      (C) is satisfactory to notarial officer.
  (2) By a verification on oath or affirmation of credible witness personally appearing before notarial officer and personally known to notarial officer.

(c) **Discretion**: Notarial officer may require a person to provide additional information or identification credentials necessary to assure notarial officer of identity of person.

LAW

308. Authority to refuse to perform notarial act.
   (a) Specific refusal. A notarial officer may refuse to perform a notarial act if the notarial officer is not satisfied that:
      (1) the individual executing the record is competent or has the capacity to execute the record;
      (2) the individual's signature is knowingly and voluntarily made;
      (3) the individual's signature on the record or statement substantially conforms to the signature on a form of identification used to determine the identity of the individual; or
      (4) the physical appearance of the individual signing the record or statement substantially conforms to the photograph on a form of identification used to determine the identity of the individual.
   (b) General refusal. A notarial officer may refuse to perform a notarial act unless refusal is prohibited by law other than this chapter.

-----

309. Signature if individual unable to sign (Reserved).

-----

310. Notarial act in this Commonwealth.
   (a) Eligible individuals. A notarial act may be performed in this Commonwealth by any of the following:
      (1) A judge of a court of record.
      (2) A clerk, prothonotary or deputy prothonotary or deputy clerk of a court having a seal.
      (3) Any of the following:
         (i) A recorder of deeds.
         (ii) A deputy recorder of deeds.

HIGHLIGHTS

308. Authority to refuse to perform notarial act
(a) **Specific refusal**: Notarial officer may refuse to perform a notarial act if notarial officer is **not** satisfied that:
   (1) person executing record is competent or has capacity to execute the record;
   (2) person's signature is knowingly and voluntarily made;
   (3) person's signature on record or statement substantially conforms to signature on a form of identification used to determine person's identity; or
   (4) physical appearance of person signing record or statement substantially conforms to photograph on a form of identification used to determine identity of person.
(b) **General refusal**. Notarial officer may refuse to perform a notarial act unless refusal is prohibited by any law.

-----

309. Signature if individual unable to sign (Reserved).

-----

310. Notarial act in this Commonwealth
(a) **Eligible individuals**: Notarial act may be performed in this Commonwealth by:
   (1) Judge of a court of record.
   (2) Clerk of court (prothonotary/deputy prothonotary or deputy clerk of a court having a seal).
   (3) Any of following:
      (i) Recorder of deeds
      (ii) Deputy recorder of deeds

LAW

      (iii) A clerk of a recorder of deeds to the extent authorized by:

          (A) section 1 of the act of May 17, 1949 (P.L.1397, No.414), entitled "An act authorizing the recorder of deeds in counties of the first class to appoint and empower clerks employed in his office to administer oaths and affirmations";

          (B) section 1312 of the act of July 28, 1953 (P.L.723, No.230), known as the Second Class County Code; or

          (C) section 1313 of the act of August 9, 1955 (P.L.323, No.130), known as The County Code.

   (4) A notary public.

   (5) A member of the minor judiciary. As used in this paragraph, the term "minor judiciary" has the meaning given in 42 Pa.C.S. § 102 (relating to definitions).

   (6) An individual authorized by law to perform a specific notarial act.

(b) Prima facie evidence. The signature and title of an individual performing a notarial act in this Commonwealth are prima facie evidence that:

   (1) the signature is genuine; and

   (2) the individual holds the designated title.

(c) Conclusive determination. The signature and title of a notarial officer described in subsection (a)(1), (2), (3), (4) or (5) conclusively establish the authority of the notarial officer to perform the notarial act.

HIGHLIGHTS

(iii) A clerk of a recorder of deeds to extent authorized by:
  (A) section 1 of act of May 17, 1949 (P.L.1397, No.414), "An act authorizing recorder of deeds in counties of first class to appoint and empower clerks employed in his office to administer oaths and affirmations";

  (B) section 1312 of act of July 28, 1953 (P.L.723, No.230), "Second Class County Code; or
  (C) section 1313 of act of August 9, 1955 (P.L.323, No.130), "The County Code".
(4) Notary.
(5) Member of minor judiciary. "Minor judiciary" has the meaning given in 42 Pa.C.S. § 102
(6) An individual authorized by law to perform a specific notarial act.

(b) **Prima facie evidence:** Signature and title of an individual performing a notarial act in this Commonwealth are prima facie evidence that:
  (1) signature is genuine; and
  (2) individual holds designated title.
(c) **Conclusive determination.** Signature and title of a notarial officer described in subsection (a)(1), (2), (3), (4) or (5) conclusively establish authority of notarial officer to perform the notarial act.

LAW

311. Notarial act in another state.
   (a) Effect. A notarial act performed in another state has the same effect under the law of this Commonwealth as if performed by a notarial officer of this Commonwealth if the act performed in that state is performed by any of the following:
      (1) A notary public of that state.
      (2) A judge, clerk or deputy clerk of a court of that state.
      (3) An individual authorized by the law of that state to perform the notarial act.
   (b) Prima facie evidence. The signature and title of an individual performing a notarial act in another state are prima facie evidence that:
      (1) the signature is genuine; and
      (2) the individual holds the designated title.
   (c) Conclusive determination. The signature and title of a notarial officer described in subsection (a)(1) or (2) conclusively establish the authority of the notarial officer to perform the notarial act.

-----

312. Notarial act under authority of federally recognized Indian tribe.
   (a) Effect. A notarial act performed under the authority and in the jurisdiction of a federally recognized Indian tribe has the same effect as if performed by a notarial officer of this Commonwealth if the act performed in the jurisdiction of the tribe is performed by any of the following:
      (1) A notary public of the tribe.
      (2) A judge, clerk or deputy clerk of a court of the tribe.
      (3) An individual authorized by the law of the tribe to perform the notarial act.

HIGHLIGHTS

311. Notarial act in another state
  (a) **Effect.** Notarial act performed in another state has <u>same effect</u> under law of this Commonwealth as if performed by a notarial officer of this Commonwealth if act performed in that state is performed by any of following:
    (1) Notary of that state.
    (2) Judge, clerk or deputy clerk of a court of that state.
    (3) An individual authorized by law of that state to perform the notarial act.
  (b) **Prima facie evidence.** <u>Signature</u> and <u>title</u> of an individual performing a notarial act in another state are prima facie evidence that:
    (1) signature is genuine; and
    (2) individual holds designated title.
  (c) **Conclusive determination.** Signature and title of a notarial officer described in subsection (a)(1) or (2) conclusively establish authority of notarial officer to perform notarial act.

-----

312. Notarial act under authority of federally recognized Indian tribe
  (a) **Effect.** Notarial act performed under authority and in jurisdiction of federally recognized Indian tribe has <u>same effect</u> as if performed by notarial officer of this Commonwealth if act performed in jurisdiction of tribe is performed by any of following:
    (1) Notary of tribe.
    (2) Judge, clerk or deputy clerk of a court of tribe.
    (3) Individual authorized by law of tribe to perform notarial act.

LAW

   (b) Prima facie evidence. The signature and title of an individual performing a notarial act under the authority of and in the jurisdiction of a federally recognized Indian tribe are prima facie evidence that:
      (1) the signature is genuine; and
      (2) the individual holds the designated title.
   (c) Conclusive determination. The signature and title of a notarial officer described in subsection (a)(1) or (2) conclusively establish the authority of the notarial officer to perform the notarial act.

-----

313. Notarial act under Federal authority.
   (a) Effect. A notarial act performed under Federal law has the same effect under the law of this Commonwealth as if performed by a notarial officer of this Commonwealth if the act performed under Federal law is performed by any of the following:
      (1) A judge, clerk or deputy clerk of a court.
      (2) An individual in military service or performing duties under the authority of military service who is authorized to perform notarial acts under Federal law.
      (3) An individual designated a notarizing officer by the United States Department of State for performing notarial acts overseas.
      (4) An individual authorized by Federal law to perform the notarial act.
   (b) Prima facie evidence. The signature and title of an individual acting under Federal authority and performing a notarial act are prima facie evidence that:
      (1) the signature is genuine; and
      (2) the individual holds the designated title.

HIGHLIGHTS

(b) **Prima facie evidence**. Signature and title of an individual performing a notarial act under authority of and in jurisdiction of a federally recognized Indian tribe are prima facie evidence that:
(1) signature is genuine; and
(2) individual holds designated title.

(c) **Conclusive determination**. Signature and title of a notarial officer described in subsection (a)(1) or (2) conclusively establish authority of notarial officer to perform notarial act.

-----

313. Notarial act under Federal authority

(a) **Effect**. Notarial act performed under Federal law has same effect under law of this Commonwealth as if performed by a notarial officer of Commonwealth if act performed under Federal law is performed by any of following:
(1) Judge, clerk or deputy clerk of a court.
(2) Individual in military service or performing duties under authority of military who is authorized to perform notarial acts under Federal law.
(3) Individual designated a notarizing officer by US Department of State for performing notarial acts overseas.
(4) Individual authorized by Federal law to perform notarial act.

(b) **Prima facie evidence**. Signature and title of a person acting under Federal authority performing a notarial act is prima facie evidence that:
(1) signature is genuine; and
(2) person holds designated title.

LAW

(c) Conclusive determination. The signature and title of notarial officer described in subsection (a)(1), (2) or (3) conclusively establish the authority of the notarial officer to perform the notarial act.

-----

314. Foreign notarial act.
- (a) (Reserved).
- (b) Effect.
    - (1) This subsection applies to a notarial act:
        - (i) performed under authority and in the jurisdiction of a foreign state or constituent unit of the foreign state; or
        - (ii) performed under the authority of a multinational or international governmental organization.
    - (2) A notarial act under paragraph (1) has the same effect under the law of this Commonwealth as if performed by a notarial officer of this Commonwealth.
- (c) Conclusive establishment. If the title of office and indication of authority to perform notarial acts in a foreign state appears in a digest of foreign law or in a list customarily used as a source for that information, the authority of an officer with that title to perform notarial acts is conclusively established.
- (d) Prima facie evidence. The signature and official stamp of an individual holding an office described in subsection (c) are prima facie evidence that:
    - (1) the signature is genuine; and
    - (2) the individual holds the designated title.

HIGHLIGHTS

(c) **Conclusive determination.** <u>Signature</u> and <u>title</u> of notarial officer described in subsection (a)(1), (2) or (3) conclusively establish authority of notarial officer to perform notarial act.

-----

314. Foreign notarial act
(a) (Reserved).
(b) **Effect.**
   (1) This subsection applies to notarial act:
      (i) performed under authority and in jurisdiction of a foreign state or constituent unit of foreign state; or
      (ii) performed under authority of a multinational or international governmental organization.
   (2) Notarial act under paragraph (1) has <u>same effect</u> under law of this Commonwealth as if performed by a notarial officer of this Commonwealth.

(c) **Conclusive establishment.** If title of office and indication of authority to perform notarial acts in a foreign state appears in a digest of foreign law or in a list customarily used as a source for that information, authority of an officer with that title to perform notarial acts is conclusively established.

(d) **Prima facie evidence.** <u>Signature</u> and <u>official stamp</u> of an individual holding an office described in subsection (c) are prima facie evidence that:
   (1) signature is genuine; and
   (2) individual holds designated title.

LAW

(e) Hague Convention.
   (1) This subsection applies to an apostille which is:
      (i) in the form prescribed by the Hague Convention of October 5, 1961; and
      (ii) issued by a foreign state party to the Hague Convention.
   (2) An apostille under paragraph (1) conclusively establishes that:
      (i) the signature of the notarial officer is genuine; and
      (ii) the notarial officer holds the indicated office.

(f) Consular authentications.
   (1) This subsection applies to a consular authentication:
      (i) issued by an individual designated by the United States Department of State as a notarizing officer for performing notarial acts overseas; and
      (ii) attached to the record with respect to which the notarial act is performed.
   (2) A consular authentication under paragraph (1) conclusively establishes that:
      (i) the signature of the notarial officer is genuine; and
      (ii) the notarial officer holds the indicated office.

(g) Definition. As used in this section, the term "foreign state" means a government other than the United States, a state or a federally recognized Indian tribe.

HIGHLIGHTS

(e) **Hague Convention**
   (1) This subsection applies to an <u>apostille</u> which is:
      (i) in the form prescribed by the Hague Convention of Oct. 5, 1961; and
      (ii) issued by a foreign state party to the Hague Convention.
   (2) An apostille under paragraph (1) conclusively establishes that:
      (i) signature of notarial officer is genuine; and
      (ii) notarial officer holds indicated office.

(f) **Consular authentications.**
   (1) This subsection applies to a consular authentication:
      (i) issued by an individual designated by US Department of State as a notarizing officer for performing notarial acts overseas; and
      (ii) attached to record with respect to which notarial act is performed.
   (2) A <u>consular authentication</u> under paragraph (1) conclusively establishes that:
      (i) signature of notarial officer is genuine; and
      (ii) the notarial officer holds the indicated office.

(g) **Definition**. As used in this section, "**foreign state**" means a government other than the US, a state or a federally recognized Indian tribe.

LAW

315. Certificate of notarial act.
  (a) Requirements.
    (1) A notarial act shall be evidenced by a certificate.
    (2) Regardless of whether the notarial officer is a notary public, the certificate must:
      (i) be executed contemporaneously with the performance of the notarial act;
      (ii) be signed and dated by the notarial officer;
      (iii) identify the county and State in which the notarial act is performed; and
      (iv) contain the title of office of the notarial officer.
    (3) If the notarial officer is a notary public, all of the following subparagraphs apply:
      (i) The notary public must:
        (A) sign the notary public's name exactly and only as it appears on the commission; or
        (B) execute the notary public's electronic signature in a manner which attributes the signature to the notary public identified in the commission.
      (ii) The certificate must indicate the date of expiration of the notarial officer's commission.
  (b) Official stamp.
    (1) If a notarial act regarding a tangible record is performed by a notary public, an official stamp shall be affixed to the certificate near the notary public's signature in a form capable of photographic reproduction
    (2) If a notarial act is performed regarding a tangible record by a notarial officer other than a notary public and the certificate contains the information specified in subsection (a)(2)(ii), (iii) and (iv), an official stamp may be affixed to the certificate.

HIGHLIGHTS

315. Certificate of notarial act
  (a) **Requirements**
   (1) A notarial act includes a **certificate**.
   (2) All certificates must:
      (i) be executed at same time as notarial act;
      (ii) be signed and dated by notarial officer;
      (iii) state county and State where notarial act is performed; and
      (iv) contain title of office of notarial officer.

   (3) If notarial officer is a notary, all of following apply:
      (i) Notary must:
         (A) sign notary's name exactly as it appears on commission; or
         (B) execute notary's electronic signature
      (ii) Certificate must indicate date of expiration of notarial officer's commission.

  (b) **Official stamp**
   (1) If a notarial act on a tangible record (paper) is performed by a notary, **an official stamp shall be affixed to certificate near notary public's signature**
   (2) If a notarial act is performed regarding a tangible record by a notarial officer other than a notary and certificate contains information specified in subsection (a)(2)(ii), (iii) and (iv), an official stamp may be affixed to certificate.

LAW

 (3) If a notarial act regarding an electronic record is performed by a notary public and the certificate contains the information specified in subsection (a)(2)(ii), (iii) and (iv) and (3), an official stamp may be attached to or logically associated with the certificate.
 (4) If a notarial act regarding an electronic record is performed by a notarial officer other than a notary public and the certificate contains the information specified in subsection (a)(2)(ii), (iii) and (iv), an official stamp may be attached to or logically associated with the certificate.
(c) Sufficiency. A certificate of a notarial act is sufficient if it meets the requirements of subsections (a) and (b) and:
 (1) is in a short form set forth in section 316 (relating to short form certificates);
 (2) is in a form otherwise permitted by a statutory provision;
 (3) is in a form permitted by the law applicable in the jurisdiction in which the notarial act was performed; or
 (4) sets forth the actions of the notarial officer and the actions are sufficient to meet the requirements of the notarial act as provided in:
  (i) sections 305 (relating to requirements for certain notarial acts), 306 (relating to personal appearance required) and 307 (relating to identification of individual); or
  (ii) a statutory provision other than this chapter.
(d) Effect. By executing a certificate of a notarial act, a notarial officer certifies that the notarial officer has complied with the requirements and made the determinations specified in sections 304 (relating to authority to perform notarial act), 305 and 306.

HIGHLIGHTS

(3) If a notarial act regarding an electronic record is performed by a notary and certificate contains information specified in subsection (a)(2)(ii), (iii) and (iv) and (3), an official stamp <u>may</u> be attached to or logically associated with certificate.

(4) If a notarial act regarding an electronic record is performed by a notarial officer other than a notary public and certificate contains information specified in subsection (a)(2)(ii), (iii) and (iv), an official stamp <u>may</u> be attached to or logically associated with certificate.

(c) **Sufficiency.** Certificate of a notarial act is sufficient if it meets requirements of subsections (a), (b) and:
   (1) is in a short form as per section 316 (short form certificates);
   (2) is in a form permitted by law;
   (3) is in a form permitted by law applicable in jurisdiction where notarial act was performed; or
   (4) sets forth actions of notarial officer and actions are sufficient to meet requirements of notarial act as in: (i) sections 305 (requirements for certain notarial acts), 306 (personal appearance required) and 307 (identification of individual); or (ii) a statutory provision other than this law.

(d) **Effect.** By executing a certificate of a notarial act, a notarial officer certifies that notarial officer has complied with requirements and made determinations specified in sections 304 (relating to authority to perform notarial act), 305 and 306.

LAW

(e) Prohibition. A notarial officer may not affix the notarial officer's signature to or logically associate it with a certificate until the notarial act has been performed.

(f) Process.
   (1) If a notarial act is performed regarding a tangible record, a certificate shall be part of or securely attached to the record.
   (2) If a notarial act is performed regarding an electronic record, the certificate shall be affixed to or logically associated with the electronic record.
   (3) If the department has established standards under section 327 (relating to regulations) for attaching, affixing or logically associating the certificate, the process must conform to the standards

-----

316. Short form certificates.

The following short form certificates of notarial acts are sufficient for the purposes indicated if completed with the information required by section 315(a) and (b) (relating to certificate of notarial act):

HIGHLIGHTS

(e) **Prohibition.** Notarial officer may <u>not</u> affix notarial officer's signature to a certificate <u>until the notarial act has been performed</u>.

(f) **Process**
   (1) If a notarial act is performed regarding a tangible record, a certificate shall be <u>part of or securely attached to record</u>.
   (2) If a notarial act is performed regarding an electronic record, certificate shall be <u>affixed to or associated with electronic record</u>.
   (3) If department has established standards under section 327 (relating to regulations) for attaching, affixing or logically associating the certificate, process must conform to standards.

-----

316. Short form certificates

The following short form certificates of notarial acts are sufficient if completed with information required by section 315(a) and (b) (relating to certificate of notarial act):

> **"SHORT FORM CERTIFICATES**
>
> The Revised Uniform Law on Notarial Acts (RULONA) requires that a notarial act must be evidenced by a certificate. This means that, when notarizing documents, the notary public must include a statement indicating the type of notarial act performed, showing when, where and before whom the notarial act was completed. It is never acceptable to place only one's signature and seal on a document, without any notarial language."
>
> *http://www.dos.pa.gov*

SHORT FORM CERTIFICATES OF NOTARIAL ACTS

(1)   Acknowledgment in an individual capacity

(2)   Acknowledgment in a representative capacity

(2.1) Acknowledgment by an attorney at law

(3)   Verification on oath or affirmation

(4)   Witnessing or attesting a signature

(5)   Certifying a copy of a record

(6)   Certifying the transcript of a deposition

ACE THE PENNSYLVANIA NOTARY PUBLIC EXAM

LAW

(1) For an acknowledgment in an individual capacity:

State of
County of

    This record was acknowledged before me on _____ (date) by _____ (name(s) of individual(s)).

Signature of notarial officer
    Stamp

Title of office
My commission expires:

-----

(2) For an acknowledgment in a representative capacity:

State of
County of

This record was acknowledged before me on _____ (date) by _____(name(s) of individual(s)) as _____(type of authority, such as officer or trustee) who represent that (he, she or they) are authorized to act on behalf of _____ (name of party on behalf of whom record was executed).

Signature of notarial officer
    Stamp

Title of office
My commission expires:

ACE THE PENNSYLVANIA NOTARY PUBLIC EXAM

HIGHLIGHTS

(1) For an acknowledgment in an individual capacity:

State of _____
County of _____

    This record was acknowledged before me on ____ (date)

by _____ (name(s) of individual(s)).

Signature of notarial officer
        Stamp

Title of office
My commission expires:

---

(2) For acknowledgment in a representative capacity:

State of _____
County of _____

This record was acknowledged before me on _____ (date)

by _____(name(s) of individual(s))

as _____(type of authority, such as officer or trustee)

who represent that (he, she or they) are authorized to act on

behalf of _____ (name of party on behalf of whom record

was executed).

Signature of notarial officer
        Stamp

Title of office
My commission expires:

ACE THE PENNSYLVANIA NOTARY PUBLIC EXAM

LAW

(2.1) For an acknowledgment by an attorney at law pursuant to 42 Pa.C.S. § 327 (relating to oaths and acknowledgments):

State of
County of

This record was acknowledged before me on _____ (date) by _____ (name of attorney) Supreme Court identification number _____ as a member of the bar of the Pennsylvania Supreme Court certified that he/she was personally present when _____ (name(s) of individual(s)) executed the record and that _____ (name(s) of individual(s)) executed the record for the purposes contained therein.

Signature of notarial officer
    Stamp

Title of office
My commission expires:

-----

(3) For a verification on oath or affirmation:

State of
County of

Signed and sworn to (or affirmed) before me on _____ (date) by _____ (name(s) of individual(s) making statement)

Signature of notarial officer
    Stamp

Title of office
My commission expires

ACE THE PENNSYLVANIA NOTARY PUBLIC EXAM

HIGHLIGHTS

(2.1) For an <u>acknowledgment by an attorney at law</u> pursuant to 42 Pa.C.S. § 327 (relating to oaths and acknowledgments):

State of _____
County of_____

This record was acknowledged before me on _____ (date)

by _____ (name of attorney) Supreme Court identification number

_____ as a member of the bar of the Pennsylvania

Supreme Court certified that he/she was personally present when

_____ (name(s) of individual(s))

executed the record and that _____ (name(s) of

individual(s)) executed the record for the purposes contained therein.

Signature of notarial officer
    Stamp

Title of office
My commission expires:

---

(3) For a <u>verification on oath or affirmation</u>:

State of _____
County of_____

Signed and sworn to (or affirmed) before me on _____ (date)

by _____ (name(s) of individual(s) making statement)

Signature of notarial officer
    Stamp

Title of office
My commission expires

ACE THE PENNSYLVANIA NOTARY PUBLIC EXAM

LAW

(4) For witnessing or attesting a signature:

State of
County of

  Signed (or attested) before me on _____ (date)
by _____ (name(s) of individual(s))

Signature of notarial officer
  Stamp

Title of office
My commission expires:

-----

(5) For certifying a copy of a record:

State of
County of

I certify that this is a true and correct copy of a _____
in the possession of _____
Dated
Signature of notarial officer
  Stamp

Title of office
My commission expires:

ACE THE PENNSYLVANIA NOTARY PUBLIC EXAM

HIGHLIGHTS

(4) For <u>witnessing or attesting a signature</u>:

```
State of _____
County of _____

    Signed (or attested) before me on _____ (date)
by _____ (name(s) of individual(s))


Signature of notarial officer
        Stamp

Title of office
My commission expires:
```

(5) For <u>certifying a copy of a record</u>:

```
State of _____
County of _____

I certify that this is a true and correct copy of a _____

in the possession of _____,


Dated

Signature of notarial officer
        Stamp

Title of office
My commission expires:
```

LAW

(6) For certifying the transcript of a deposition:

State of
County of

I certify that this is a true and correct copy of the transcript of the deposition of _____
Dated
Signature of notarial officer
Stamp

Title of office:
My commission expires:

HIGHLIGHTS

(6) For <u>certifying the transcript of a deposition:</u>

State of _____
County of _____

I certify that this is a true and correct copy of the transcript of the deposition of _____

Dated

Signature of notarial officer
Stamp

Title of office:
My commission expires:

LAW

317. Official stamp.

The following shall apply to the official stamp of a notary public:

    (1) A notary public shall provide and keep an official seal, which shall be used to authenticate all the acts, instruments and attestations of the notary public. The seal must be a rubber stamp and must show clearly in the following order:

        (i) The words "Commonwealth of Pennsylvania."

        (ii) The words "Notary Seal."

        (iii) The name as it appears on the commission of the notary public and the words "Notary Public."

        (iv) The name of the county in which the notary public maintains an office.

        (v) The date the notary public's commission expires.

        (vi) Any other information required by the department.

    (2) The seal must have a maximum height of one inch and width of three and one-half inches, with a plain border.

    (3) The seal must be capable of being copied together with the record to which it is affixed or attached or with which it is logically associated.

-----

318. Stamping device.

(a) Security.

    (1) A notary public is responsible for the security of the stamping device of the notary public. A notary public may not allow another individual to use the device to perform a notarial act.

    (2) On resignation of a notary public commission or on the expiration of the date set forth in the stamping device, the notary public shall disable the stamping device by destroying, defacing, damaging, erasing or securing it against use in a manner which renders it unusable.

HIGHLIGHTS

317. Official stamp
The following shall apply to the official stamp of a notary:
  (1) Notary shall provide and keep an **official seal**,
      to be used to authenticate all acts, instruments and
      attestations of notary.
      Seal must be a <u>rubber stamp</u> and must show
      clearly in the following order:
      (i) The words "<u>Commonwealth of Pennsylvania</u>."
      (ii) The words "<u>Notary Seal</u>."
      (iii) Name <u>as it appears on commission</u> of
          the notary and the words "<u>Notary Public</u>."
      (iv) Name of <u>county</u> where notary maintains an office.
      (v) Date notary's commission <u>expires</u>.
      (vi) Any other information required by department.
  (2) Seal must have a maximum height of <u>one inch
      and width of three and one-half inches</u>, with a plain
      border.
  (3) Seal must be capable of being copied together
      with record to which it is affixed or attached.

-----

318. Stamping device
(a) Security
  (1) A notary is responsible for security of notary
      stamping device. Notary may <u>not</u> allow another
      person to use device to perform a notarial act.
  (2) On resignation of a notary commission or on
      expiration of date set forth in stamping device,
      notary shall disable stamping device by destroying,
      defacing, damaging, erasing or securing it against
      use in a manner which renders it unusable.

LAW

(2.1) An individual whose notary commission has been suspended or revoked shall surrender possession of the stamping device to the department.

(3) On the death or adjudication of incompetency of a notary, the personal representative or guardian of the notary public or any person knowingly in possession of the stamping device shall render it unusable by destroying, defacing, damaging, erasing or securing it against use in a manner which renders it unusable.

(b) Loss or theft. If a stamping device is lost or stolen, the notary public or the personal representative or guardian of the notary public shall notify the department promptly upon discovering that the device is lost or stolen.

-----

319. Journal.

(a) Maintenance. A notary public shall maintain a journal in which the notary public records in chronological order all notarial acts that the notary public performs.

(b) Format. A journal may be created on a tangible medium or in an electronic format. A notary public may maintain a separate journal for tangible records and for electronic records. If the journal is maintained on a tangible medium, it shall be a bound register with numbered pages. If the journal is maintained in an electronic format, it shall be in a tamper-evident electronic format complying with the regulations of the department.

(c) Entries. An entry in a journal shall be made contemporaneously with performance of the notarial act and contain all of the following information:

(1) The date and time of the notarial act.

(2) A description of the record, if any, and type of notarial act.

HIGHLIGHTS

(2.1) An individual whose notary commission has been suspended or revoked shall surrender possession of stamping device to department.

(3) On death or adjudication of incompetency of a notary, personal representative or guardian of notary or any person knowingly in possession of stamping device shall render it unusable by destroying, defacing, damaging, erasing or securing it against use in a manner which renders it unusable.

(b) **Loss or theft.** If a stamping device is lost or stolen, notary or personal representative or guardian of notary shall notify department promptly upon discovering that device is lost or stolen.

-----

319. Journal

(a) **Maintenance** A notary shall maintain a journal in which notary records in chronological order all notarial acts that notary performs.

(b) **Format**. Journal may be created on a tangible medium or in an electronic format. Notary may maintain a separate journal for tangible records and for electronic records. If journal is maintained on a tangible medium, it shall be a bound register with numbered pages. If journal is maintained in an electronic format, it shall be in a tamper-evident electronic format complying with regulations of department.

(c) **Entries**. An entry in a journal shall be made contemporaneously with performance of notarial act and contain all of following information:
  (1) Date and time of notarial act.
  (2) A description of record, if any, and type of notarial act.

LAW

    (3) The full name and address of each individual for whom the notarial act is performed.
    (4) If identity of the individual is based on personal knowledge, a statement to that effect.
    (5) If identity of the individual is based on satisfactory evidence, a brief description of the method of identification and any identification credential presented, including the date of issuance and expiration of an identification credential.
    (6) The fee charged by the notary public.
(d) Loss or theft. If a journal is lost or stolen, the notary public shall promptly notify the department on discovering that the journal is lost or stolen.
(e) Termination of office. A notary public shall deliver the journal of the notary public to the office of the recorder of deeds in the county where the notary public last maintained an office within 30 days of:
    (1) expiration of the commission of the notary public, unless the notary public applies for a commission within that time period;
    (2) resignation of the commission of the notary public; or
    (3) revocation of the commission of the notary public.
(f) Repository. (Reserved).
(g) Death or incompetency. On the death or adjudication of incompetency of a current or former notary public, the personal representative or guardian of the notary public or a person knowingly in possession of the journal of the notary public shall deliver it within 30 days to the office of the recorder of deeds in the county where the notary public last maintained an office.
(g.1) Certified copies. A notary public shall give a certified copy of the journal to a person that applies for it.
(h) Protection.
    (1) A journal and each public record of the notary public are exempt from execution.
    (2) A journal is the exclusive property of the notary

HIGHLIGHTS

(3) Full name and address of each individual for whom notarial act is performed.
(4) If identity of individual is based on personal knowledge, a statement to that effect.
(5) If identity of individual is based on satisfactory evidence, a brief description of method of identification and any identification credential presented, including date of issuance and expiration of an identification credential.
(6) Fee charged by notary.

(d) **Loss or theft**. If a journal is lost or stolen, notary shall promptly notify department.

(e) **Termination of office**. Notary shall deliver journal of notary to office of recorder of deeds in county where notary last maintained an office within 30 days of:
  (1) expiration of commission of notary, unless notary public applies for a commission within that time;
  (2) resignation of commission of notary; or
  (3) revocation of commission of notary.

(f) **Repository**. (Reserved).

(g) **Death or incompetency**. On death or adjudication of incompetency of current or former notary, personal representative or guardian of notary or a person knowingly in possession of journal of notary shall deliver it within 30 days to office of recorder of deeds in county where notary last maintained an office.

(g.1) **Certified copies**. A notary shall give a certified copy of journal to a person that applies for it.

(h) **Protection**
  (1) The journal and each public record of the notary are exempt from execution.
  (2) A journal is exclusive property of notary.

LAW

(3) A journal may not be:
   (i) used by any person other than the notary public; or
   (ii) surrendered to an employer of the notary public upon termination of employment

-----

320. Notification regarding performance of notarial act on electronic record; selection of technology.
(a) Selection. A notary public may select one or more tamper-evident technologies to perform notarial acts with respect to electronic records. A person may not require a notary public to perform a notarial act with respect to an electronic record with a technology that the notary public has not selected.
(b) Notice and approval.
   (1) Before a notary public performs the initial notarial act with respect to an electronic record, a notary public shall notify the department that the notary public will be performing notarial acts with respect to electronic records and identify each technology the notary public intends to use.
   (2) If the department has established standards for approval of technology under section 327 (relating to regulations), the technology must conform to the standards. If the technology conforms to the standards, the department shall approve the use of the technology.

HIGHLIGHTS

(3) A journal may <u>not</u> be:
   (i) used by any person other than notary; or
   (ii) surrendered to an employer of notary upon termination of employment

-----

320. Notification regarding performance of notarial act on electronic record; selection of technology

(a) **Selection**. Notary may select one or more tamper-evident technologies to perform notarial acts with respect to electronic records. Person may not require notary to perform a notarial act with respect to an electronic record with a technology that notary has not selected.

(b) **Notice and approval**

   (1) Before a notary performs initial notarial act with respect to an electronic record, notary shall notify department that notary will be performing notarial acts with respect to electronic records and identify each technology he intends to use.

   (2) If department has established standards for approval of technology under section 327 (relating to regulations), technology must conform to standards. If technology conforms to standards, department shall approve use of technology.

LAW

321. Appointment and commission as notary public; qualifications; no immunity or benefit.

(a) Eligibility. An applicant for appointment and commission as a notary public must meet all of the following:
   (1) Be at least 18 years of age.
   (2) Be a citizen or permanent legal resident of the United States.
   (3) Be a resident of or have a place of employment or practice in this Commonwealth.
   (4) Be able to read and write English.
   (5) Not be disqualified to receive a commission under section 323 (relating to sanctions).
   (6) Have passed the examination required under section 322(a) (relating to examination, basic education and continuing education).
   (7) Comply with other requirements established by the department by regulation as necessary to insure the competence, integrity and qualifications of a notary public and to insure the proper performance of notarial acts.

(b) Application. An individual qualified under subsection (a) may apply to the department for appointment and commission as a notary public. The application must comply with all of the following:
   (1) Be made to the department on a form prescribed by the department.
   (2) Be accompanied by a nonrefundable fee of $42, payable to the Commonwealth of Pennsylvania. This amount shall include the application fee for notary public commission and fee for filing of the bond with the department.
   (3) (Deleted by amendment.)

(c) Oath or affirmation. Upon appointment and before issuance of a commission as a notary public, an applicant must execute an oath or affirmation of office.

HIGHLIGHTS

321. Appointment and commission as notary; qualifications; no immunity or benefit.

(a) **Eligibility**. Applicant for appointment and commission as a notary must meet all of following:
  (1) At least 18 years of age.
  (2) A citizen or permanent legal resident of the US.
  (3) A resident of or have a place of employment or practice in this Commonwealth.
  (4) Able to read and write English.
  (5) Not be disqualified to receive a commission under section 323 (relating to sanctions).
  (6) Have passed the examination required under section 322(a) (relating to examination, basic education and continuing education).
  (7) Comply with requirements established by department by regulation as necessary to insure competence, integrity and qualifications of a notary and to insure proper performance of notarial acts.

(b) **Application**. Individual qualified under subsection (a) may apply to department for appointment and commission as a notary. Application must comply with all of following:
  (1) Be made to department on a form prescribed by the department.
  (2) Be accompanied by a nonrefundable fee of $42, payable to Commonwealth of Pennsylvania. Amount shall include application fee for notary commission and fee for filing of bond with department.
  (3) (Deleted by amendment.)

(c) **Oath or affirmation** Upon appointment and before issuance of a commission, an applicant must execute an oath or affirmation of office.

LAW

(d) Bond.
   (1) Within 45 days after appointment and before issuance of a commission as a notary public, the applicant must obtain a surety bond in:
      (i) the amount of $10,000; or
      (ii) the amount set by regulation of the department.
   (2) (Reserved).
   (3) The bond must:
      (i) be executed by an insurance company authorized to do business in this Commonwealth;
      (ii) cover acts performed during the term of the notary public commission; and
      (iii) be in the form prescribed by the department.
   (4) If a notary public violates law with respect to notaries public in this Commonwealth, the surety or issuing entity is liable under the bond.
   (5) The surety or issuing entity must give 30 days' notice to the department before canceling the bond.
   (6) The surety or issuing entity shall notify the department not later than 30 days after making a payment to a claimant under the bond.
   (7) A notary public may perform notarial acts in this Commonwealth only during the period in which a valid bond is on file with the department.

(d.1) Official signature.
   (1) The official signature of each notary public shall be registered, for a fee of 50¢, in the "Notary Register" provided for that purpose in the prothonotary's office of the county where the notary public maintains an office within:
      (i) 45 days after appointment or reappointment; and
      (ii) 30 days after moving to a different county.
   (2) In a county of the second class, the official signature of each notary public shall be registered in the office of the clerk of courts within the time periods specified in paragraph (1).

HIGHLIGHTS

(d) **Bond**
   (1) Within 45 days after appointment and before issuance of a commission, applicant must obtain a surety bond in:
     (i) amount of $10,000; or
     (ii) amount set by regulation of department.
   (2) (Reserved).
   (3) Bond must:
     (i) be executed by an insurance company authorized to do business in Commonwealth;
     (ii) cover acts performed during term of notary commission; and
     (iii) be in form prescribed by department.
   (4) If notary violates a notary public law of this Commonwealth, surety or issuing entity is liable under the bond.
   (5) Surety or issuing entity must give 30 days' notice to department before canceling bond.
   (6) Surety or issuing entity shall notify department not later than 30 days after making a payment to a claimant under the bond.
   (7) A notary may perform notarial acts in this Commonwealth only during period in which a valid bond is on file with department.

(d.1) **Official signature**
   (1) Official signature of each notary shall be registered, for a fee of 50¢, in the "Notary Register" provided for that purpose in prothonotary's office of county where notary maintains an office within:
     (i) 45 days after appointment or reappointment; and
     (ii) 30 days after moving to a different county.
   (2) In a county of second class, official signature of each notary shall be registered in office of clerk of courts within time periods specified in paragraph (1).

LAW

(d.2) Recording and filing.
- (1) Upon appointment and prior to entering into the duties of a notary public, the bond, oath of office and commission must be recorded in the office of the recorder of deeds of the county in which the notary public maintains an office.
- (2) Upon reappointment, the bond, oath of office and commission must be recorded in the office of the recorder of deeds of the county in which the notary public maintains an office.
- (3) Within 90 days of recording under this subsection, a copy of the bond and oath of office must be filed with the department.

(e) Issuance. On compliance with this section, the department shall issue to an applicant a commission as a notary public for a term of four years.

(f) Effect.
- (1) A commission to act as a notary public authorizes a notary public to perform notarial acts. If a notary public fails to comply with subsection (d.1) or (d.2), the notary public's commission shall be null and void.
- (2) A commission to act as a notary public does not provide a notary public any immunity or benefit conferred by law of this Commonwealth on public officials or employees

HIGHLIGHTS

(d.2) **Recording and filing**
  (1) Upon appointment and prior to entering into duties of notary, notary must record bond, oath of office and commission in office of recorder of deeds of county in which notary maintains an office.

  (2) Upon reappointment, bond, oath of office and commission must be recorded in office of recorder of deeds of county where notary maintains an office.

  (3) Within 90 days of recording under this subsection, a copy of bond and oath of office must be filed with the department.

(e) **Issuance** On compliance with this section, department shall issue to an applicant a commission as a notary for a term of 4 years.

(f) **Effect**
  (1) A commission to act as a notary authorizes a notary to perform notarial acts. If a notary fails to comply with preceding subsection (d.1) or (d.2), notary public's commission shall be null and void.

  (2) A commission to act as a notary does not provide a notary any immunity or benefit conferred by law of this Commonwealth on public officials or employees.

LAW

322. Examination, basic education and continuing education.

(a) Examination. An applicant for a commission as a notary public who does not hold a commission in this Commonwealth must pass an examination administered by the department or an entity approved by the department. The examination must be based on the course of study described in subsection (b).

(b) Basic education. An applicant under subsection (a) must, within the six-month period immediately preceding application, complete a course of at least three hours of notary public basic education approved by the department. For approval, the following apply:
  (1) The course must cover the statutes, regulations, procedures and ethics relevant to notarial acts, with a core curriculum including the duties and responsibilities of the office of notary public and electronic notarization.
  (2) The course must either be interactive or classroom instruction.

(c) Continuing education. An applicant for renewal of appointment and commission as a notary public must, within the six-month period immediately preceding application, complete a course of at least three hours of notary public continuing education approved by the department. For approval, the following apply:
  (1) The course must cover topics which ensure maintenance and enhancement of skill, knowledge and competency necessary to perform notarial acts.
  (2) The course must either be interactive or classroom instruction.

(d) Preapproval. All basic and continuing education courses of study must be preapproved by the department.

HIGHLIGHTS

322. Examination, basic education and continuing education

(a) **Examination**. Notary applicant who does not hold a commission in this Commonwealth must pass an examination administered by department or an entity approved by the department. Examination must be based on course of study described in subsection (b).

(b) **Basic education.** The applicant must, within 6-month period preceding application, complete at least a 3-hours course of basic education approved by the department. The following apply:

   (1) Course must cover statutes, regulations, procedures and ethics relevant to notarial acts, with a core curriculum including duties and responsibilities of the office of notary and electronic notarization.
   (2) Course must be interactive or classroom instruction.

(c) **Continuing education**. Applicant for renewal of appointment and commission as a notary must, within the 6-month period immediately preceding application, complete a course of at least 3-hours of notary continuing education approved by department. The following apply:
   (1) Course must cover topics which ensure maintenance and enhancement of skill, knowledge and competency necessary to perform notarial acts.
   (2) Course must be interactive or classroom instruction.

(d) **Preapproval**. Basic and continuing education courses of study must be preapproved by department.

LAW

323. Sanctions.
(a) Authority. The department may deny, refuse to renew, revoke, suspend, reprimand or impose a condition on a commission as notary public for an act or omission which demonstrates that the individual lacks the honesty, integrity, competence or reliability to act as a notary public. Such acts or omissions include:
   (1) Failure to comply with this chapter.
   (2) A fraudulent, dishonest or deceitful misstatement or omission in the application for a commission as a notary public submitted to the department.
   (3) Conviction of or acceptance of Accelerated Rehabilitative Disposition by the applicant or notary public for a felony or an offense involving fraud, dishonesty or deceit.
   (4) A finding against or admission of liability by the applicant or notary public in a legal proceeding or disciplinary action based on the fraud, dishonesty or deceit of the applicant or notary public.
   (5) Failure by a notary public to discharge a duty required of a notary public, whether by this chapter, by regulation of the department or by Federal or State law.
   (6) Use of false or misleading advertising or representation by a notary public representing that the notary public has a duty, right or privilege that the notary public does not have.
   (7) Violation by a notary public of a regulation of the department regarding a notary public.
   (8) Denial, refusal to renew, revocation, suspension or conditioning of a notary public commission in another state.
   (9) Failure of a notary public to maintain a bond under section 321(d) (relating to appointment and commission as notary public; qualifications; no immunity or benefit).

HIGHLIGHTS

323. Sanctions
(a) **Authority**. Department may deny, refuse to renew, revoke, suspend, reprimand or impose a condition on a commission because of an act or omission which demonstrates that individual lacks the honesty, integrity, competence or reliability to act as a notary. Such acts or omissions include:
(1) Failure to comply with this law.
(2) Fraudulent, dishonest or deceitful misstatement or omission in application for a commission as a notary submitted to department.
(3) Conviction of or acceptance of Accelerated Rehabilitative Disposition by applicant or notary for a felony or an offense involving fraud, dishonesty or deceit.
(4) Finding against or admission of liability by applicant or notary in a legal proceeding or disciplinary action based on fraud, dishonesty or deceit of applicant or notary.
(5) Failure by a notary to discharge a duty required of a notary, whether by this law, by regulation of department or by Federal or State law.

(6) Use of false or misleading advertising or representation by a notary representing that notary has a duty, right or privilege notary does not have.

(7) Violation by a notary of a regulation of department regarding a notary.
(8) Denial, refusal to renew, revocation, suspension or conditioning of a notary commission in another state.

(9) Failure of a notary to maintain a bond under section 321(d) (relating to appointment and commission as notary; qualifications; no immunity or benefit).

LAW

(a.1) Administrative penalty. The department may impose an administrative penalty of up to $1,000 on a notary public for each act or omission which constitutes a violation of this chapter or on any person who performs a notarial act without being properly appointed and commissioned under this chapter.

(b) Administrative Agency Law. Action by the department under subsection (a) or (a.1) is subject to 2 Pa.C.S. Chs. 5 Subch. A (relating to practice and procedure of Commonwealth agencies) and 7 Subch. A (relating to judicial review of Commonwealth agency action).

(c) Other remedies. The authority of the department under this section does not prevent a person from seeking and obtaining other criminal or civil remedies provided by law.

(d) Investigations and hearings.

    (1) The department may issue a subpoena, upon application of an attorney responsible for representing the Commonwealth in disciplinary matters before the department, for the purpose of investigating alleged violations of the disciplinary provisions administered by the department.

    (2) In an investigation or hearing, the department, as it deems necessary, may subpoena witnesses, administer oaths, examine witnesses, take testimony and compel the production of documents.

    (3) The department may apply to Commonwealth Court under 42 Pa.C.S. § 761(a)(2) (relating to original jurisdiction) to enforce a subpoena under this subsection.

(e) Other enforcement authority. The department may initiate civil proceedings at law or in equity to force the requirements of this chapter and to enforce regulations or orders issued under this chapter. In addition, the department may request the prosecution of criminal

HIGHLIGHTS

(a.1) **Administrative penalty**. Department may impose an administrative penalty of up to $1,000 on a notary for each act or omission which constitutes a violation of this law or on any person who performs a notarial act without being properly appointed and commissioned under this law.

(b) **Administrative Agency Law. Action by department** under subsection (a) or (a.1) is subject to 2 Pa.C.S. Chs. 5 Subch. A (relating to practice and procedure of Commonwealth agencies) and 7 Subch. A (relating to judicial review of Commonwealth agency action).

(c) **Other remedies**. Authority of department under this section does not prevent person from seeking and obtaining other criminal or civil remedies provided by law.

(d) **Investigations and hearings**
  (1) Department may issue a subpoena, upon application of an attorney responsible for representing Commonwealth in disciplinary matters before department, for purpose of investigating alleged violations of disciplinary provisions administered by department.
  (2) In an investigation or hearing, department, as it deems necessary, may subpoena witnesses, administer oaths, examine witnesses, take testimony and compel production of documents.
  (3) Department may apply to Commonwealth Court under 42 Pa.C.S. § 761(a)(2) (relating to original jurisdiction) to enforce a subpoena under this subsection.

(e) **Other enforcement authority**. Department may initiate civil proceedings at law or in equity to force requirements of this law and to enforce regulations or orders issued under this law. In addition, department may request prosecution of criminal

LAW

offenses to the extent provided by this chapter or as otherwise provided by law relating to notaries public, notarial officers or notarial acts, in the manner provided by the act of October 15, 1980 (P.L.950, No.164), known as the Commonwealth Attorneys Act.

(f) Criminal penalties applicable. The following apply:
  (1) Except as provided in this chapter or otherwise provided by law, it is unlawful for a person to hold himself out as a notary public or as a notarial officer or to perform a notarial act.
  (2) Falsely pretending to be a notary public or a notarial officer and performing any action in furtherance of such false pretense shall subject the person to the penalties set forth in 18 Pa.C.S. § 4913 (relating to impersonating a notary public or a holder of a professional or occupational license).
  (3) The use of an official stamp by a person who is not a notary public named on the stamp shall constitute a violation of 18 Pa.C.S. § 4913.
  (4) Except as provided in paragraph (2) or (3), any person violating this chapter or a regulation of the department commits a summary offense and shall, upon conviction, be sentenced to pay a fine of not more than $1,000.

324. Database of notaries public.
The department shall maintain an electronic database of notaries public:
(1) through which a person may verify the authority of a notary public to perform notarial acts; and
(2) which indicates whether a notary public has notified the department that the notary public will be performing notarial acts on electronic records.

HIGHLIGHTS

offenses to extent provided by this law or as otherwise provided by law relating to notaries public, notarial officers or notarial acts, in the manner provided by the act of Oct. 15, 1980 (P.L.950, No.164), known as the Commonwealth Attorneys Act.
(f) **Criminal penalties applicable**. The following apply:
  (1) Except as provided in this law or otherwise provided by law, it is unlawful for a person to hold himself out as a notary or as a notarial officer or to perform a notarial act.
  (2) Falsely pretending to be a notary or a notarial officer and performing any action in furtherance of such false pretense shall subject person to penalties in 18 Pa.C.S. § 4913 (relating to impersonating a notary or holder of a professional or occupational license).
  (3) Use of an official stamp by a person who is not a notary named on the stamp shall constitute a violation of 18 Pa.C.S. § 4913.
  (4) Except as provided in paragraph (2) or (3), any person violating this chapter or a regulation of the department commits a summary offense and shall, upon conviction, be sentenced to pay a fine of not more than $1,000.

324. **Database of notaries public**
Department shall maintain an electronic database of notaries public:
(1) through which a person may verify authority of a notary to perform notarial acts; and
(2) which indicates whether a notary has notified department that notary will be performing notarial acts on electronic records.

LAW

325. Prohibited acts.
(a) No authority. A commission as a notary public does not authorize the notary public to:
   (1) assist persons in drafting legal records, give legal advice or otherwise practice law;
   (2) act as an immigration consultant or an expert on immigration matters;
   (3) represent a person in a judicial or administrative proceeding relating to immigration to the United States, United States citizenship or related matters; or
   (4) receive compensation for performing any of the activities listed in this subsection.
(b) False advertising. A notary public may not engage in false or deceptive advertising.
(c) Designation.
   (1) Except as set forth in paragraph (2), a notary public may not use the term "notario" or "notario publico."
   (2) Paragraph (1) does not apply to an attorney at law.
(d) Representations.
   (1) Except as set forth in paragraph (2), the following apply:
      (i) A notary public may not advertise or represent that the notary public may:
         (A) assist persons in drafting legal records;
         (B) give legal advice; or
         (C) otherwise practice law.
      (ii) If a notary public advertises or represents that the notary public offers notarial services, whether orally or in a record, including broadcast media, print media and the Internet, the notary public shall include the following statement, or an alternate statement authorized or required by the department, in the advertisement or representation, prominently and in each language used in the advertisement or representation:

HIGHLIGHTS

325. Prohibited acts

(a) **No authority**. A commission as a notary does not authorize the notary to:
   (1) assist persons in drafting legal records, give legal advice or otherwise practice law;
   (2) act as an immigration consultant or an expert on immigration matters;
   (3) represent a person in a judicial or administrative proceeding relating to immigration to the US, US citizenship, or related matters; or
   (4) receive compensation for performing any of activities listed in this subsection.

(b) **False advertising**. A notary may not engage in false or deceptive advertising.

(c) **Designation**.
   (1) Except as set forth in paragraph (2), a notary may **not** use the term "notario" or "notario publico."
   (2) Paragraph (1) does not apply to an attorney at law.

(d) **Representations**.
   (1) Except as in paragraph (2), the following apply:
      (i) A notary may not advertise or represent that notary may:
         (A) assist persons in drafting legal records;
         (B) give legal advice; or
         (C) otherwise practice law.
      (ii) If a notary advertises or represents that notary offers notarial services, whether orally or in a record, including broadcast media, print media and the Internet, notary shall include following statement, or an alternate statement authorized or required by the department, in the advertisement or representation, prominently and in each language used in advertisement or representation:

LAW

> I am not an attorney licensed to practice law in this Commonwealth. I am not allowed to draft legal records, give advice on legal matters, including immigration, or charge a fee for those activities.

   (iii) If the form of advertisement or representation is not broadcast media, print media or the Internet and does not permit inclusion of the statement required by this subsection because of size, it shall be displayed prominently or provided at the place of performance of the notarial act before the notarial act is performed.

   (2) Paragraph (1) does not apply to an attorney at law.

(e) Original records. Except as otherwise allowed by law, a notary public may not withhold access to or possession of an original record provided by a person that seeks performance of a notarial act by the notary public.

(f) Crimes Code. There are provisions in 18 Pa.C.S. (relating to crimes and offenses) which apply to notaries public.

-----

326. Validity of notarial acts.

(a) Failures. Except as otherwise provided in section 304(b) (relating to authority to perform notarial act), the failure of a notarial officer to perform a duty or meet a requirement specified in this chapter does not invalidate a notarial act performed by the notarial officer.

(b) Invalidation. The validity of a notarial act under this chapter does not prevent an aggrieved person from seeking to invalidate the record or transaction which is the subject of the notarial act or from seeking other remedies based on Federal law or the law of this Commonwealth other than this chapter.

(c) Lack of authority. This section does not validate a purported notarial act performed by an individual who does not have the authority to perform notarial acts.

HIGHLIGHTS

> I am not an attorney licensed to practice law in this Commonwealth. I am not allowed to draft legal records, give advice on legal matters, including immigration, or charge a fee for those activities.

    (iii) If the form of advertisement or representation is not broadcast media, print media or the Internet and does not permit inclusion of the statement required by this subsection because of size, it shall be displayed prominently or provided at the place of performance of the notarial act before the notarial act is performed.

  (2) Paragraph (1) does not apply to an attorney at law.

(e) **Original records**. Except as otherwise allowed by law, a notary may not withhold access to or possession of an original record provided by a person that seeks performance of a notarial act by the notary.

(f) **Crimes Code**. There are provisions in 18 Pa.C.S. (relating to crimes and offenses) which apply to notaries public.

-----

326. Validity of notarial acts

(a) **Failures**. Except as otherwise provided in section 304(b) (relating to authority to perform notarial act), failure of a notarial officer to perform a duty or meet a requirement specified in this chapter does not invalidate a notarial act performed by the notarial officer.

(b) **Invalidation**. Validity of notarial act under this chapter does not prevent an aggrieved person from seeking to invalidate record or transaction which is subject of notarial act or from seeking other remedies under Federal law or the law of this Commonwealth other than this law.

(c) **Lack of authority**. This section does not validate a purported notarial act performed by an individual who does not have authority to perform notarial acts.

ACE THE PENNSYLVANIA NOTARY PUBLIC EXAM

LAW

327. Regulations.
(a) Authority. Except as provided in section 329.1(a) (relating to fees of notaries public), the department may promulgate regulations to implement this chapter. Regulations regarding the performance of notarial acts with respect to electronic records may not require or accord greater legal status or effect to the implementation or application of a specific technology or technical specification. Regulations may:
   (1) Prescribe the manner of performing notarial acts regarding tangible and electronic records.
   (2) Include provisions to ensure that any change to or tampering with a record bearing a certificate of a notarial act is self-evident.
   (3) Include provisions to ensure integrity in the creation, transmittal, storage or authentication of electronic records or signatures.
   (4) Prescribe the process of granting, renewing, conditioning, denying, suspending or revoking a notary public commission and assuring the trustworthiness of an individual holding a commission as notary public.
   (5) Include provisions to prevent fraud or mistake in the performance of notarial acts.
   (6) Establish the process for approving and accepting surety bonds under section 321(d) (relating to appointment and commission as notary public; qualifications; no immunity or benefit).
   (7) Provide for the administration of the examination under section 322(a) (relating to examination, basic education and continuing education) and the course of study under section 322(b).
   (7.1) Require applicants for appointment and commission as notaries public to submit criminal history record information as provided in 18 Pa.C.S. Ch. 91 (relating to criminal history record information)

HIGHLIGHTS

327. Regulations

(a) **Authority**. Except as provided in section 329.1(a) (fees of notaries public), department may promulgate regulations to implement this law. Regulations regarding performance of notarial acts with respect to electronic records may not require or accord greater legal status or effect to implementation or application of a specific technology or technical specification. Regulations may:

  (1) Prescribe manner of performing notarial acts regarding tangible and electronic records.
  (2) Include provisions to ensure that any change to or tampering with a record bearing a certificate of a notarial act is self-evident.
  (3) Include provisions to ensure integrity in creation, transmittal, storage or authentication of electronic records or signatures.
  (4) Prescribe process of granting, renewing, conditioning, denying, suspending or revoking a notary commission and assuring trustworthiness of an individual holding a commission as notary.
  (5) Include provisions to prevent fraud or mistake in performance of notarial acts.
  (6) Establish process for approving and accepting surety bonds under section 321(d) (relating to appointment and commission as notary; qualifications; no immunity or benefit).
  (7) Provide for administration of the examination under section 322(a) (relating to examination, basic education and continuing education) and course of study under section 322(b).
  (7.1) Require applicants for appointment and commission as notaries public to submit criminal history record information as provided in 18 Pa.C.S. Ch. 91 (criminal history record information)

LAW

      as a condition of appointment.
   (8) Include any other provision necessary to implement this chapter.
(b) Considerations. In promulgating regulations about notarial acts with respect to electronic records, the department shall consider, so far as is consistent with this chapter:
   (1) the most recent standards regarding electronic records promulgated by national bodies, such as the National Association of Secretaries of State;
   (2) standards, practices and customs of other states which substantially enact the Revised Uniform Law on Notarial Acts; and
   (3) the views of governmental officials and entities and other interested persons.

-----

328. Notary public commission in effect.
A commission as a notary public in effect on the effective date of this chapter continues until its date of expiration. A notary public who applies to renew a commission as a notary public on or after the effective date of this chapter is subject to this chapter. A notary public, in performing notarial acts after the effective date of this chapter, shall comply with this chapter.

-----

329. Savings clause.
This chapter does not affect the validity or effect of a notarial act performed before the effective date of this chapter.

HIGHLIGHTS

　　　as a condition of appointment.
　(8) Include any other provision necessary to implement this chapter.
(b) **Considerations**. In promulgating regulations about notarial acts with respect to electronic records, department shall consider:
　(1) most recent standards regarding electronic records promulgated by national bodies, such as National Association of Secretaries of State;
　(2) standards, practices and customs of other states which substantially enact the Revised Uniform Law on Notarial Acts; and
　(3) the views of governmental officials and entities and other interested persons.

-----

328. Notary public commission in effect
Commission as a notary in effect on effective date of this law continues until its date of expiration. A notary who applies to renew a commission as a notary on or after effective date of this law is subject to this law. A notary, in performing notarial acts after the effective date of this law, shall comply with this law.

-----

329. Savings clause
This law does not affect the validity or effect of a notarial act performed before the effective date of this law.

LAW

329.1. Fees of notaries public.

(a) Department.--The fees of notaries public shall be fixed by the department by regulation.

(b) Prohibition.--A notary public may not charge or receive a notary public fee in excess of the
fee fixed by the department.

(c) Operation

(1) The fees of the notary public shall be separately stated.

(2) A notary public may waive the right to charge a fee.

(3) Unless paragraph (2) applies, a notary public shall:

(i) display fees in a conspicuous location in the place of business of the notary public; or

(ii) provide fees, upon request, to a person utilizing the services of the notary public.

(d) Presumption.--The fee for a notary public:

(1) shall be the property of the notary public; and

(2) unless mutually agreed by the notary public and the employer, shall not belong to or
be received by the entity that employs the notary public.

330. Uniformity of application and construction.

In applying and construing this chapter, consideration must be given to the need to promote uniformity of the law with respect to its subject matter among states that enact it.

331. Relation to Electronic Signatures in Global and National Commerce Act.

To the extent permitted by section 102 of the Electronic Signatures in Global and National Commerce Act (Public Law 106-229, 15 U.S.C. § 7002), this chapter may modify or supersede provisions of that act.

2013, Oct. 9, P.L. 609, No. 73, § 2, effective 180 days after published notice of 57 Pa.C.S.A. § 322 course approval. Amended 2014, July 9, P.L. 1035, No. 119, § 1, effective 180 days after published notice of 57 Pa.C.S.A. § 322 course approval.

Notice of course approval published on April 29, 2017 at 47 Pa.B. 2518. Effective date is 180 days after publication of this notice (October 26, 2017).

HIGHLIGHTS

329.1. Fees of notaries public
(a) **Department**. Fees of notaries are fixed by the department by regulation.
(b) **Prohibition**. Notary may not charge or receive a notary fee greater than fee fixed by the department.

(c) **Operation**
  (1) Fees of a notary shall be separately stated.
  (2) A notary may waive right to charge a fee.
  (3) Unless paragraph (2) applies, a notary public shall:
     (i) display fees in a conspicuous location in place of business of the notary; or
     (ii) provide fees, upon request, to a person utilizing services of the notary.
(d) **Presumption**. Fee for a notary:
  (1) shall be the property of the notary public; and
  (2) unless mutually agreed by notary and employer, fees shall not belong to or be received by the employer of the notary public.

330. Uniformity of application and construction
In applying and construing this law, consideration must be given to need to promote uniformity of the law with respect to its subject matter among states that enact it.

331. Relation to Electronic Signatures in Global and National Commerce Act.
To extent permitted by section 102 of the Electronic Signatures in Global and National Commerce Act (Public Law 106-229, 15 U.S.C. § 7002), this law may modify or supersede provisions of that act.

LAW

NOTARIES PUBLIC (57 PA.C.S.) - OMNIBUS AMENDMENTS
Act of Jul. 9, 2014, P.L. 1035, No. 119   Cl. 57
Session of 2014
No. 2014-119

SB 1001

AN ACT

Amending Title 57 (Notaries Public) of the Pennsylvania Consolidated Statutes, in revised uniform law on notarial acts, further providing for appointment and commission as notary public, qualifications and no immunity or benefit and for regulations; and further providing for application for appointment to the office of notary public.

The General Assembly of the Commonwealth of Pennsylvania hereby enacts as follows:

Section 1. Section 321(b) and (d.2) of Title 57 of the Pennsylvania Consolidated Statutes are amended to read:

§ 321. Appointment and commission as notary public; qualifications; no immunity or benefit.
* * *
(b) Application.--An individual qualified under subsection (a) may apply to the department for appointment and commission as a notary public. The application must comply with all of the following:
(1) Be made to the department on a form prescribed by the department.
(2) Be accompanied by a nonrefundable fee of $42, payable to the Commonwealth of Pennsylvania. This amount shall include the application fee for notary public commission and fee for filing of the bond with the department.

HIGHLIGHTS

NOTARIES PUBLIC (57 PA.C.S.) - OMNIBUS AMENDMENTS
Act of Jul. 9, 2014, P.L. 1035, No. 119   Cl. 57
Session of 2014
No. 2014-119

SB 1001

AN ACT

Amending Title 57 (Notaries Public) of the Pennsylvania Consolidated Statutes, in revised uniform law on notarial acts, further providing for appointment and commission as notary public, qualifications and no immunity or benefit and for regulations; and further providing for application for appointment to the office of notary public.

The General Assembly of Commonwealth of Pennsylvania enacts as follows:

Section 1. Section 321(b) and (d.2) of Title 57 of the Pennsylvania Consolidated Statutes are amended to read:

321. Appointment and commission as notary public; qualifications; no immunity or benefit
* * *

(b) Application. An individual qualified under subsection
    (a) may apply to department for appointment and commission as a notary public. The application must comply with all of following:
      (1) Be made to the department on a form prescribed by the department.
      (2) Be accompanied by a nonrefundable fee of $42, payable to the Commonwealth of Pennsylvania. This amount shall include the application fee for notary public commission and fee for filing of the bond with department.

LAW

(3) Bear an endorsement as follows:
(i) Except as set forth in this paragraph, the endorsement of the senator of the district in which the applicant resides.
(ii) If the applicant does not reside in this Commonwealth, the endorsement of the senator of the district in which the applicant is employed.
(iii) If there is a vacancy in the senatorial district under subparagraph (i) or (ii), the endorsement of the senator of an adjacent district.]
* * *

(d.2) Recording and filing.
(1) [Upon] Within 45 days after appointment and prior to entering into the duties of a notary public, the bond, oath of office and commission must be recorded in the office of the recorder of deeds of the county in which the notary public maintains an office.
(2) Upon reappointment, the bond, oath of office and commission must be recorded in the office of the recorder of deeds of the county in which the notary public maintains an office.
(3) Within 90 days of recording under this subsection, a copy of the bond and oath of office must be filed with the department.
* * *

Section 2. Section 327(a) of Title 57 is amended by adding a paragraph to read:
§ 327. Regulations.
(a) Authority.--Except as provided in section 329.1(a)(relating to fees of notaries public), the department may promulgate regulations to implement this chapter. Regulations regarding the performance of notarial acts with respect to electronic records may not require or accord greater legal status or effect to the implementation or application of a specific technology or technical specification.

HIGHLIGHTS

(3) Bear an endorsement as follows:
(i) Except as set forth in this paragraph, the endorsement of the senator of the district in which the applicant resides.
(ii) If the applicant does not reside in this Commonwealth, the endorsement of the senator of the district in which the applicant is employed.
(iii) If there is a vacancy in the senatorial district under subparagraph (i) or (ii), the endorsement of the senator of an adjacent district.] (Repealed)
* * *

(d.2) Recording and filing.
(1) **Within 45 days** after appointment and prior to entering into duties of a notary public, the bond, oath of office and commission must be recorded in office of the recorder of deeds of county in which notary public maintains an office.

(2) **Upon reappointment**, notary must record bond, oath of office and commission in the office of the recorder of deeds of county in which notary public maintains an office.

(3) **Within 90 days** of recording, a copy of the bond and oath of office must be filed with the department.

* * *

Section 2. Section 327(a) of Title 57 is amended by adding a paragraph to read:
327. Regulations
(a) Authority. Except as in section 329.1(a)(fees of notaries public), the department may promulgate regulations to implement this law. Regulations regarding performance of notarial acts with respect to electronic records may not require or accord greater legal status or effect to implementation or application of a specific technology or technical specification.

LAW

Regulations may:
* * *
(7.1) Require applicants for appointment and commission as notaries public to submit criminal history record information as provided in 18 Pa.C.S. Ch. 91 (relating to criminal history record information) as a condition of appointment.
* * *

Section 3. Notwithstanding section 5(a) of the act of August 21, 1953 (P.L.1323, No.373), known as The Notary Public Law, an application for appointment to the office of notary public shall not be required to bear:
(1) the endorsement of the Senator of the district in which the applicant for appointment to the office of notary public resides; or
(2) if the applicant for appointment to the office of notary public does not reside in this Commonwealth, the endorsement of the Senator of the district in which the applicant is employed.
Section 4. This act shall take effect as follows:
(1) This section shall take effect immediately.
(2) The addition of 57 Pa.C.S. § 327(a)(7.1) shall take effect immediately.
(3) Section 3 of this act shall take effect in 180 days.
(4) The remainder of this act shall take effect 180 days after publication of the notice under section 4 of the act of October 9, 2013 (P.L.609, No.73), entitled "An act amending Titles 42 (Judiciary and Judicial Procedure) and 57 (Notaries Public) of the Pennsylvania Consolidated Statutes, enacting uniform laws on attestation in the areas of unsworn foreign declarations and notarial acts; making editorial changes; making related repeals; and abrogating a regulation," or immediately, whichever is later.
APPROVED--The 9th day of July, A.D. 2014.

HIGHLIGHTS

Regulations may:
* * *
(7.1) Require applicants for appointment and commission as notaries public to submit criminal history record information as provided in 18 Pa.C.S. Ch. 91 (criminal history record information) as a condition of appointment.
* * *

Section 3. Notwithstanding section 5(a) of the act of August 21, 1953 (P.L.1323, No.373), known as The Notary Public Law, **an application for appointment to the office of notary public shall NOT be required to bear:**
(1) the endorsement of the Senator of the district in which the applicant for appointment to the office of notary public resides; or
(2) if the applicant for appointment to the office of notary public does not reside in this Commonwealth, the endorsement of the Senator of the district in which the applicant is employed. (N/A)

Section 4. This act shall take effect as follows:
(1) This section shall take effect immediately.
(2) The addition of 57 Pa.C.S. § 327(a)(7.1) shall take effect immediately.
(3) Section 3 of this act shall take effect in 180 days.
(4) The remainder of this act shall take effect 180 days after publication of the notice under section 4 of the act of October 9, 2013 (P.L.609, No.73), entitled "An act amending Titles 42 (Judiciary and Judicial Procedure) and 57 (Notaries Public) of the Pennsylvania Consolidated Statutes, enacting uniform laws on attestation in the areas of unsworn foreign declarations and notarial acts; making editorial changes; making related repeals; and abrogating a regulation," or immediately, whichever is later.
APPROVED--The 9th day of July, A.D. 2014.

Uniform Acknowledgment Act(*)

(Act No. 188, approved July 24, 1941, as amended by Acts 353 and 354 of 1947, Act 3 of 1951, Act 58 of 1957, Act 61 of 1961 and Act 71 of 1981)

AN ACT

Relating to acknowledgments of written instruments, and to make uniform the law with relation thereto.

The General Assembly of the Commonwealth of Pennsylvania hereby enacts as follows:

Section 1. Acknowledgment of Instruments.
Any instruments may be acknowledged in the manner and form now provided by the laws of this State or as provided by this act.

Section 2. Acknowledgment within this State.
The acknowledgment of any instrument may be made in this State before:
(1) A judge of a court of record;
(2) A clerk, prothonotary or deputy prothonotary or deputy clerk of a court having a seal;
(3) A recorder of deeds or deputy recorder of deeds;
(4) A notary public;
(5) A justice of the peace, magistrate or alderman.

Section 3. Acknowledgment within the United States.
The acknowledgment of any instrument may be made without the State, but within the United States, or territory or insular possession of the United States, or in the District of Columbia, and within the jurisdiction of the officer before:
(1) A clerk or deputy of any federal court;
(2) A clerk, prothonotary or deputy prothonotary or deputy clerk of any court of record of any state or other jurisdiction;

(*) Formatted for clarity.

(3) A notary public;
(4) A recorder of deeds.

Section 4. Acknowledgment outside the US.
The acknowledgment of any instrument may be made without the US before
> (1) an ambassador, minister, charge d' affaires, counselor to or secretary of a legation, consul general, consul, vice-consul, commercial attaché or consular agent of the US accredited to the country where acknowledgment is made;
> (2) a notary public of the country where acknowledgment is made;
> (3) a judge or clerk of a court of record of the country where acknowledgment is made.

Section 5. Requisites of Acknowledgment.
Officer taking acknowledgment shall know or have satisfactory evidence that person making acknowledgment is person described in and who executed the instrument.

Section 6. Acknowledgment by Married Women
An acknowledgment of a married woman may be made in the same form as though she were unmarried.

Section 7. Forms of Certificates
An officer taking the acknowledgment shall endorse thereon or attach thereto a certificate substantially in one of the following forms:

(1) By individuals

State of _____
County of _____

On this, the _____ day of _____, 19____, before me _____, the undersigned officer, personally appeared _____, known to me (or satisfactorily proven) to be the person(s) whose name(s) is/are subscribed to the within instrument, and acknowledged that _____ executed the same for the purposes therein contained.

In witness whereof, I hereunto set my hand and official seals.

_____
_____
Title of Officer

(2) By a Corporation

State of _____
County of _____
    On this, the _____ day of _____, 19____, before me _____, the undersigned officer, personally appeared _____, who acknowledged himself to be the _____ of _____, a corporation, and that he as such _____, being authorized to do so, executed foregoing instrument for the purpose therein contained by signing the name of the corporation by himself as _____
    In witness whereof, I hereunto set my hand and official seals.

_____
_____
                               Title of Officer

Any deed, conveyance, mortgage or other instrument in writing, made and executed by a corporation, may be acknowledged by any officer of said corporation whose signature appears on such deed, conveyance, mortgage or other instrument in writing, in execution or in attestation of the execution thereof.

(3) By an attorney in fact

State of _____
County of _____
    On this, the _____ day of _____, 19____, before me _____, the undersigned officer, personally appeared _____, known to me (or satisfactorily proven) to be the person whose name is subscribed as attorney in fact for _____, and acknowledged that he executed the same as the act of his principal for the purposes therein contained. In witness whereof, I hereunto set my hand and official seals.

                                    _____

                                    Title of Officer

(4) By any public official or deputy thereof or by any trustee, administrator, guardian, or executor

State of _____

County of _____

    On this, the _____ day of _____, 19____, before me _____, the undersigned officer, personally appeared _____, of the State (County or City as the case may be) of _____, known to me (or satisfactorily proven) to be the person described in the foregoing instrument, and acknowledged that he executed the same in the capacity therein stated and for the purposes therein contained.

    In witness whereof, I hereunto set my hand and official seals.

_____

_____

Title of Officer

(5) By any attorney-at-law

State of _____

County of _____

     On this, the _____ day of _____, 19____, before me _____, the undersigned officer, personally appeared _____, known to me (or satisfactorily proven) to be a member of the bar of the highest court of said state and a subscribing witness to the within instrument and certified that he was personally present when _____, whose name(s) is/are subscribed to the within instrument executed the same, and that said persons acknowledge that _____ executed the same for the purposes therein contained.

     In witness whereof, I hereunto set my hand and official seals.

_____

_____

Title of Officer

Section 8. Execution of Certificate. The certificate of the acknowledging officer shall be completed by his signature, his official seal, if he has one, the title of his office, and, if he is a notary public, the date his commission expires.

Section 9. Authentication of Acknowledgments.
(1) If the acknowledgment is taken within this State, or if taken without this State by an officer of this State, or is made without the United States by an officer of the United States, no authentication shall be necessary.

(2) If the acknowledgment is taken without this State, but in the United States, a territory or insular possession of the United States, or the District of Columbia, no authentication shall be necessary if the official before whom the acknowledgment is taken affixes his official seal to the instrument so acknowledged; otherwise the certificate shall be authenticated by a certificate as to the official character of such officer, executed (1) if the acknowledgment is taken by a clerk or deputy clerk of court, by the presiding judge of the court, or (2) if the acknowledgment is taken by some other authorized officer, by the official having custody of the official record of the election, appointment or commission of the officer taking such acknowledgment.

Section 10. Acknowledgments under Laws of other States. Notwithstanding any provision in this act contained, the acknowledgment of any instrument without this State in compliance with the manner and form prescribed by the laws of the place of its execution, if in a state, territory or insular possession of the United States, or in the District of Columbia, verified by the official seal of the officer before whom it is acknowledged or authenticated, in the manner provided by section 9, subsection 2 hereof, shall have the same effect as an acknowledgment in the manner and form prescribed by the laws of this State for instruments executed within the State.

Section 10.1. Acknowledgment by persons Serving in or with the Armed Forces of the United States.
In addition to the acknowledgment of instruments in the manner and form and as otherwise now and hereafter authorized by the laws of this State or by this Act, persons serving in or with the Armed Forces of the United States or their dependents wherever located may acknowledge the same before any commissioned officer in active service of the armed forces of the United States with the rank of Second Lieutenant or higher in the Army, Air Force, or Marine Corps or Ensign or higher in the Navy or Coast Guard. The instrument shall not be rendered invalid by the failure to state therein the place of execution or acknowledgment. No authentication of the officer's certificate of acknowledgment shall be required but the officer taking the acknowledgment shall endorse thereon or attach thereto a certificate substantially in the following form: (See next page.)

Section 11. Acknowledgments not Affected by this Act. No acknowledgment heretofore taken shall be affected by anything contained herein.

Section 12. Uniformity of Interpretation. This act shall be so interpreted as to make uniform the laws of those States which enact it.

Section 13. Name of Act. This act may be cited as the Uniform Acknowledgment Act.

Section 14. Time of Taking Effect. This act shall take effect immediately upon final enactment.

Section 10.1. Acknowledgment by persons Serving in or with the Armed Forces of the United States.

> On this the _____ day of _____, 19___ before me _____ the undersigned officer personally appeared _____ (Serial No.)(if any) known to me (or satisfactorily proven) to be (serving in or with the armed forces of the United States) [a dependent of _____ (Serial No.) (if any) a person serving in or with the armed forces of the United States] and to be the person whose name is subscribed to the within instrument and acknowledged that he executed the same for the purposes therein contained. And the undersigned does further certify that he is at the date of this certificate a commissioned officer of the rank stated below and is in the active service of the armed forces of the United States.
>
> _____
> Signature of the Officer
>
> _____
> Rank and Serial No. of Officer
> and Command to which attached

RULONA REGULATIONS - Proposed August 2016
Selected Edited Sections

The following are edited sections of RULONA **Regulations**, that have additional details which supplement parts of the preceding law sections.

161.2 (d) A notary public may not charge any fee for notarizing the supporting affidavit required in an Emergency Absentee Ballot or the affidavit of a person needing assistance to vote an absentee ballot.

167.2 A post office box number is not a sufficient address for Department of State records.

167.11. Eligibility for appointment and commission. Applicants not residing in Pennsylvania
(a) If an applicant is not a resident of Pennsylvania, the applicant must have a place of employment or practice in this Commonwealth.
(b) Employment or practice in this Commonwealth shall be on an ongoing basis.

167.13. Eligibility for appointment and commission deemed resignation
If a notary public neither resides nor works in the Commonwealth, that notary public shall be deemed to have resigned from the office of notary public as of the date the residency ceases or employment within the Commonwealth terminates.
A notary public who resigns that notary's commission in accordance with this section shall notify the Department of State in writing or electronically within 30 days of the effective date of the resignation.

67.14 (d) The applicant's signature on the application must match the applicant's name as provided on the application.
The applicant shall use a legible, recognizable handwritten signature, which can be attributed to the applicant by anyone examining or authenticating the signature.

If an applicant's preferred signature is not legible and recognizable, the applicant must also legibly print his or her name immediately adjacent to his or her preferred signature. For the purposes of this subsection, a signature is legible and recognizable if it is distinct, easily readable and understandable, and the notary's full name may be clearly discerned by looking at the signature

167.18. Notification of Change in Information
(a) Notary public must notify Department of State within **30 days of any change in the information on file** with the Department, including the notary's:
- (1) Legal Name
- (2) Office address (includes place of employment or practice in Pennsylvania, if not a resident of the Commonwealth)
- (3) Home address
- (4) Name of electronic notarization vendor
- (5) Voluntary resignation

(b) Such notice may be made in writing or electronically and shall state the effective date of such change.

(c) Notice of a change in legal name on file with the Department shall be on a form prescribed by the Department and accompanied by evidence of the name change (such as marriage certificate, court order, divorce decree).

(d) Notice of a change in legal name on file with the Department shall also be made to the recorder of deeds of the county in which the notary public maintains an office.

167.21. Official stamp
(a) The official stamp of a notary public must show clearly in the following order:
- (1) Words "Commonwealth of Pennsylvania – Notary Seal."
- (2) The name as it appears on the commission of the notary and the words "Notary Public."
- (3) Name of county in which notary public maintains an office.
- (4) The date the notary's current commission expires.
- (5) The seven-digit commission identification number assigned by the Department.

(b) No words or terms on the official stamp may be abbreviated.

(c) The official stamp or notary seal shall be stamped or affixed to the notarial certificate near the notary's signature or attached to or logically associated with an electronic record containing the notary's signature.

(d) A notary public shall not place an imprint of the notary's official stamp over any signature in a record to be notarized or over any writing in a notarial certificate.

(e) A notary public shall not alter or deface the official stamp.

(f) A notary public shall not use the notary public's official stamp for any purpose other than to perform a notarial act.

(g) A notary public shall not permit any other person to use the notary public's official stamp for any purpose.

(h) A notary public shall not use any other notary public's official stamp or any other object in lieu of the notary's own official stamp to perform a notarial act.

(i) Transitional provision (Not applicable)

Example of Notary Public stamp:

> Commonwealth of Pennsylvania - Notary Seal
> John Q. Doe, Notary Public
> Dauphin County
> My commission expires May 19, 2019
> Commission number 1234567

167.22. Stamping device

(a) A stamping device, as used in section 302 and section 318 of Title 57 of the Pennsylvania Consolidated Statutes, does not include a non-inking embosser or crimper.

(b) A stamping device must be capable of affixing or logically associating the official stamp, such that the record to which the official stamp is so affixed or associated may be copied, filmed, scanned, or otherwise legibly reproduced.

(c) The stamping device is the exclusive property of the notary public. When not in use, the stamping device shall be kept in a secure location and accessible only to the notary. A secure location includes in the notary's sole possession or in a locked location to which only the notary has access.

d) Notification of loss or theft of stamping device under section 318(b) shall be made in writing or electronically to the Department within <u>ten days</u> after the date the notary public or personal representative or guardian discovers that the stamping device was lost, misplaced, stolen or is otherwise unavailable. The notification shall include:

(1) A statement of whether the stamping device is lost, misplaced, stolen or is otherwise unavailable;

(2) The date the notary public discovered that the official stamping

device was lost, misplaced, stolen or is otherwise unavailable;
(3) A statement that the notary public does not possess the stamping device and does not know who possesses it or where it is located;
(4) A statement that if the notary public subsequently reacquires possession of the lost, misplaced, stolen or otherwise unavailable stamping device, then the notary shall file a statement with the Department within ten days after the date the notary public reacquires possession of the lost, misplaced, stolen or otherwise unavailable stamping device;
(5) If a notary public subsequently reacquires possession of a lost, misplaced, or stolen stamping device, then the notary public shall file with the Department a written statement of explanation within ten days after the date the notary public reacquires possession of the lost, misplaced or stolen stamping device.
(6) An individual whose notary public commission has been suspended or revoked shall deliver the stamping device to the Department of State within ten days after notice of the suspension or revocation from the Department.

167. 23. Embosser
(a) A notary public may use an embossed or crimped image in the performance of a notarial act, but only in conjunction with the use of an official stamp.
(b) A notary public shall not place the embossing or crimping over any signature or printed material in a record to be notarized, or over any signature or printed material in a notarial certificate.
(c) A notary public shall not use any other notary public's embosser or any other object in lieu of the notary public's official stamp to perform a notarial act.

167.31. Identification of Notary in Journal
(a) Each journal of a notary public, whether maintained on a tangible medium or in an electronic format, shall contain the following information in any order:
  (1) The name of the notary public as it appears on commission;
  (2) The notary public's commission number;
  (3) The notary public's commission expiration date;
  (4) The notary public's office address of record with Department;
  (5) A statement that, in the event of the decease of the notary public, the journal shall be delivered or mailed to the office of the recorder of deeds in the country where the notary last maintained an office;
  (6) The meaning of any not commonly abbreviated word or symbol used in recording a notarial act in the notarial journal;
  (7) The signature of the notary public;

(b) If a notary public's name, commission expiration date, or address changes before the notary public ceases to use the notarial journal, the notary public shall add the new information after the old information and the date which the information changed.

167.32. Journal Entries

(a) Each notarial act shall be indicated as a separate entry in the journal.

(b) Optional entries. In addition to the entries required by section 319(c) of the Act, a notary journal may contain the signature of the individual for whom the notarial act is performed and any additional information about a specific transaction which might assist the notary to recall the transaction.

(c) Prohibited entries. A notary journal may not contain any personal financial or identification information about the notary's clients, such as complete Social Security numbers, complete drivers' license numbers or complete account numbers. Terminal numbers for these types of numbers, including the last four digits of a Social Security number, may be used to clarify which individual or account was involved.

(d) Fees. Each notarial fee charged should correspond to the notarial act performed.
If a fee is waived or not charged, the notary public shall indicate this fact in the journal entry, using "n/c" or "0" (zero) or a similar notation.
Clerical and administrative fees, if charged, must be separately itemized in the journal.

(e) Address. For purpose of journal entries, address means the city and state only.

(f) For the purpose of subsection (c) (Prohibited entries), "personal financial or identification information" means:

   (1) An individual's first name or first initial and last name in combination with and linked to any one or more of the following data elements when the data elements are not encrypted or redacted:
     (i) Social Security number.
     (ii) Driver's license number or a State identification card number issued in lieu of a driver's license.
     (iii) Financial account number, credit or debit card number, in combination with any required security code, access code or password that would permit access to an

individual's financial account.
(2) The term does not include publicly available information that is lawfully made available to the general public from Federal, State or local government records.

167.33. Form and Content of Notary Journal Maintained on a Tangible Medium

(a) A journal of a notary public maintained on paper or on any other tangible medium may be in any form that meets the physical requirements set out in this rule and the entry requirements set out in section 319(c) of the Act.
(b) The cover and pages inside the cover shall be bound together by any binding method that is designed to prevent the insertion, removal or substitution of the cover or a page. This includes glue, staples, grommets or another binding, but does not include the use of tape, paperclips or binder clips.
(c) Each page shall be consecutively numbered from the beginning to the end of the journal. If a journal provides two pages on which to record the required information about the same notarial act, then both pages may be numbered with the same number or each page may be numbered with a different number. A page number shall be preprinted.
(d) Each line (or entry if the journal is designed with numbered entry blocks) shall be consecutively numbered from the beginning to the end of the page. If a line extends across two pages, the line shall be numbered with the same number on both pages. A line or entry number shall be preprinted.

167.34. Form and Content of an **Electronic** Notarial Journal

(a) A journal of a notary public maintained in electronic format may be in any form that meets the requirements set out in this rule and the entry requirements set out in section 319(c) of the Act.
(b) A journal of a notary public maintained in electronic format shall be designed to prevent the insertion, removal or substitution of an entry.
(c) A journal of a notary public maintained in electronic format shall be securely stored and recoverable in the event of a hardware or software malfunction.
(d) Entries from the notarial journal must be available upon demand by the Department in a PDF format.
(e) If a signature of a signer is contained in an electronic notarial

journal, the signature must be:
(1) Attached to or logically associated with the electronic journal.
(2) Linked to the data in such a manner that any subsequent alterations to the electronic notarial journal entry are detectable and may invalidate the electronic notarial journal entry.
(f) A journal of a notary public maintained in electronic format which is delivered to the office of the recorder of deeds in compliance with section 319(e) of the Act shall be delivered in a format prescribed by the receiving recorder of deeds.

167.35. Notification of Lost or Stolen Journal
(a) A notary shall maintain custody and control of the notary journal at all times during the duration of the notary's commission.
(b) RULONA Regulations 167.21

Each page of the notary journal shall be consecutively numbered from the beginning to the end of the journal. The notification shall include:
(1) A statement of whether the notary journal is lost, misplaced, stolen or is otherwise unavailable;
(2) An explanation of how the notary journal became unavailable;
(3) The date the notary public discovered that the notary journal was lost, misplaced, stolen or is otherwise unavailable; A statement that the notary public does not possess the journal and does not know who possesses it or where it is located;
(4) A statement that if the notary public subsequently reacquires possession of the lost, misplaced, stolen or otherwise unavailable journal, then the notary public shall file a statement with the Department within ten days after the date the notary public reacquires possession of the lost, misplaced, or stolen journal;
(c) If a notary public subsequently reacquires possession of a lost, misplaced, or stolen journal, then the notary public shall file with the Department a written statement of explanation within ten days after the date the notary public reacquires possession of the lost, misplaced, stolen or otherwise unavailable journal.

167.36. Certified copies of notary journal

(a) **General. Requests for certified copies of a notary journal** made in accordance with section 319(g.1) of the Act shall be reasonable in scope and specify the particular entry or time period sought. Such requests may, but are not required to be, in writing. The notary public shall provide the certified copy within **10 days** of receipt of the request. The notary may charge reasonable fees for copying and postage, but the requestor should be advised in advance of these fees. If the scope of the request is not clear, the notary may offer to have the requester inspect the journal at the notary's office to identify the specific pages or dates that the requester is seeking.

(b) **Subpoenas and investigative requests**. A request for certified copies of a notary journal made through an investigative request by law enforcement or by the Department or in a subpoena in course of criminal or civil litigation shall be complied with in manner specified in the request or subpoena.

167.41 The name of a notary public shall consist of:

(i) a first personal name (first name), additional name(s) or initial(s) (middle name or initial), and surname (family or last name);
(ii) a first name and last name, omitting the middle name or middle initial; (iii) a first initial, middle name and last name. Neither initials alone nor nicknames will be accepted on the application or as part of the signature required on a notarial act.

(c) The name of a notary public may include suffixes such as Junior, Senior, II, III, IV or any abbreviations thereof. The name of a notary public may not include prefixes, suffixes or titles such as "Doctor," "Reverend" or "Esquire" or any abbreviations thereof.

167.43 (c) <u>A notary shall not notarize his or her own signature, nor the signature of his or her spouse.</u>

167.47. Identification of individual appearing before notarial officer – Satisfactory evidence

(a) General
(1) For the purposes of section 307(b)(1)(i), a notarial officer may rely upon:

(i) A passport or passport card issued by the United States Department of State which is current and unexpired;
(ii) A passport issued by a foreign government, which is current and unexpired, provided it uses letters, characters and a language that are read, written and understood by the notarial officer;
(iii) A driver's license or nondriver identification card issued by a state of the US, which is current and unexpired; or
(iv) A driver's license or nondriver identification card issued by a state or territory of Canada or Mexico, which is current and unexpired, provided it uses letters, characters and a language that are read, written and understood by the notarial officer.
(2) For the purposes of 307(b)(1)(ii), other forms of government identification must be current, contain the signature or photograph of the individual to be identified and must be satisfactory to the notarial officer. Current means having an issue date which is prior to the notarial act.
(3) For the purposes of section 307(b)(1)(ii), other forms of government identification may include:
(i) Identification card issued by any branch of the U.S. armed forces
(ii) An inmate identification card issued by the Pennsylvania Department of Corrections for an inmate who is currently in the custody of the Department
(iii) An identification card issued by the U.S. Department of Homeland Security
(iv) Social Security card
(v) Medicare card
(vi) Pennsylvania state and state-related university identification card

(b) Credible Witness.
(1) The identity of the individual appearing before the notarial officer can be established by the oath of a single credible witness personally known to the notary and who personally knows the document signer.
(2) A credible witness may not have a direct or pecuniary interest with respect to the record being notarized.
(3) The credible witness must make a verification on oath or affirmation that each of the following is true:
(i) The individual appearing before the notary public as the signer of the document is the person named in the

document;
(ii) The credible witness personally knows the signer;
(iii) The credible witness reasonably believes that the circumstances of the signer are such that it would be very difficult or impossible for the signer to obtain another form of identification;
(iv) The signer does not possess any of the identification documents authorized by law to establish the signer's identity; and
(v) The credible witness does not have a direct or pecuniary interest in the record being notarized.

167.48. Language and use of interpreter
(a) A notarial officer must be able to communicate directly with the individual for whom a notarial act is being performed in a language they both understand or indirectly through an interpreter who is physically present with the signer and notary at the time of the notarization and communicates directly with the individual and the notary in a language the interpreter understands.

(b) The certificate of notarial act must be worded and completed using only letters, characters and a language that are read, written and understood by the notarial officer.

(c) A notarial officer may perform a notarial act on a document that is a translation of a document that is in a language that the notarial officer does not understand only if the person performing the translation signs a verification on oath or affirmation stating that the translation is accurate and complete. The notarized translation and verification shall be attached to the document and shall comply with the Act and these regulations relating to certificate of notarial act.

167.50. Notarizing documents which contain blank spaces
(a) A notary public may not perform a notarial act with respect to a record which is designed to provide information within blank spaces, where:
  (1) The missing information has not been entered into a blank space; or
  (2) The signature of an individual signing the record is not present, unless the individual is signing in the presence

of the notary.
(b) For the purpose of subsection (a)(1), the missing information does not include:
   (1) Any empty space with N/A or a line drawn through it; or
   (2) Any additional signature lines designated for additional signers, if it is clear that the notarial act does not apply to the blank signature lines.
(c) A notarial officer performing a notarial act on nomination petitions or nomination papers with remaining empty lines for signatures should mark a line through those blank spaces for signatures, or an "X" across the blank signatures, to prevent the later addition of signatures after the notarization.

167.51. Employer-employee relationship

Notwithstanding that an individual who holds a notary commission is responsible for exercising the duties and responsibilities of the notary commission, an employer, pursuant to an agreement with an employee who is or seeks to become a notary public, may pay for the education, testing, application or bond and the cost of any stamps, seals, or other supplies required in connection with the appointment, commission, or performance of the duties of such notary public. Such agreement may also provide for the remission of fees collected by such notary public to the employer, for the increased compensation of the notary public for the amount of notary fees collected and for reimbursement of the costs of obtaining a commission should the employee or employer terminate the employment.

167.52. Limitation on provision of notarial services

Notwithstanding any other provision of law, an employer of a notary public may limit, during the employee's ordinary course of employment, the providing of notarial services by the employee solely to transactions directly associated with the business purposes of the employer.

167.61. Acknowledgments

(a) The individual making the acknowledgment shall appear personally before the notarial officer.

(b) The notarial officer shall have personal knowledge or satisfactory evidence of the identity of the individual making the acknowledgment.

(c) A record may be signed in the notarial officer's presence or a record may be signed prior to the acknowledgment. A record may not be signed subsequent to an acknowledgment.

(d) If the record is signed prior to appearance before the notarial officer, the individual making the acknowledgment shall acknowledge that the signature on the record is his or her own voluntary act.

(e) The notarial officer shall compare the signature on the record to the signature of the individual on the identification presented.

167.62. Oaths and affirmations

(a) The individual taking the oath or affirmation shall appear personally before the notarial officer.

(b) The notarial officer shall have personal knowledge or satisfactory evidence of the identity of the individual taking the oath or affirmation.

(c) An oath or affirmation may be verbal or in writing. If in writing, the oath or affirmation shall be signed in the presence of the notarial officer.

(d) In administering an oath or affirmation, the notarial officer shall require the individual taking the oath to voluntarily swear or affirm that the statements contained in the oath are true or that the individual will perform an act or duty faithfully and truthfully.

167.63. Verifications on oath or affirmation

(a) The individual making the verification on oath or affirmation shall appear personally before the notarial officer.

(b) The notarial officer shall have personal knowledge or satisfactory evidence of the identity of the individual making the verification on oath or affirmation.

(c) A record containing a statement which is being verified on oath or affirmation must be signed in the notarial officer's presence. A record containing a statement which is being verified may not be signed subsequent to the verification on oath or affirmation.

(d) The notarial officer shall compare the signature on the statement verified to the signature of the individual on the identification presented.

(e) In taking a verification on oath or affirmation, the notarial officer shall administer an oath to the individual making the statement and require that the individual voluntarily swear or affirm that the statements contained in the record are true.

167.64. Witnessing or attestation of signatures
(a) The individual signing the record shall appear personally before the notarial officer.

(b) The notarial officer shall have personal knowledge or satisfactory evidence of the identity of the individual signing the record.

(c) A record containing a signature which is being witnessed or attested must be signed in the notarial officer's presence. A record containing a signature which is being witnessed or attested may not be signed subsequent to the witnessing or attestation of the signature.

(d) The notarial officer shall compare the signature on the record signed to the signature of the individual on the identification presented.

(e) The notarial act of witnessing or attesting a signature differs from an acknowledgment in that the party relying on the record may know for certain that the record was signed on the same date that the notarial officer affixed the official seal and signature to the document.

(f) The act of witnessing a signature differs from a verification on oath or affirmation in that the signer is merely signing the record, not swearing or affirming that the contents of the record are true.

167.65. Certified or attested copies and depositions

(a) The notarial officer must be presented with the record, which may be in the possession of the requestor, or in the case where there is an official repository of records, in the care and possession of the notarial officer who may be the custodian of the official archive or collection.

(b) For paper records, the notarial officer shall compare the original document to a photocopy made by the requestor or by the notarial officer to determine that the photocopy or duplicate is a complete and accurate transcription or reproduction of the original record.

(c) For electronic records, the notarial officer shall compare the original record to a copy made by the requestor or by the notarial officer to determine that the copy is a complete and accurate transcription or reproduction of the original record.

(d) The notarial officer shall examine the record for alteration or tampering and to ensure that the original record itself is not a photocopy or copy.

(e) In issuing a certified or attested copy, the notary public does not guarantee the authenticity of the original document, its contents or its effects.

(f) Records for which a notary may not issue a certified copy include:
  (1) Vital Records (birth and death certificates)
  (2) U.S. Naturalization Certificates
  (3) Any government-issued record which on its face states "do not copy," "illegal to copy" or words of similar meaning
  (4) Any record which is prohibited by law to copy or certify

(g) Subject to subsections (f)(4) and (h), records for which a notary may issue a certified copy include:
  (1) Public records
  (2) Passports
  (3) Drivers' licenses
  (4) Transcripts
  (5) Diplomas
  (6) Contracts

(7) Leases
(8) Bills of sale
(9) Medical records, consents or waivers
(10) Powers of attorney

(h) For purpose of this section, a public record is defined as any record that is filed in or issued by a domestic or international federal, state or local government agency. If the record is intended to be sent overseas and will require an apostille or certification from the U.S. Department of State or Pennsylvania Department of State, the record must be certified by the office where the original or official copy of the record is maintained or by the public official who issued the record.
Examples include deeds, marriage records, court orders and corporate documents filed with a state office or state repository as the official record.

167.66. Protests of negotiable instrument

(a) A protest is a certificate of dishonor made by a United States consul or vice consul, or a notary public or other person authorized to administer oaths by the law of the place where dishonor occurs. It may be made upon information satisfactory to that person. The protest must:
  (1) Identify the negotiable instrument;
  (2) Certify either that presentment has been made or, if not made, the reason why it was not made, and
  (3) State that the instrument has been dishonored by nonacceptance or nonpayment.

(b) The protest may also certify that notice of dishonor has been given to some or all parties.

(c) The individual requesting the protest shall appear personally before the notarial officer and be identified in the protest as the holder of the dishonored negotiable instrument.

(d) The notarial officer shall have personal knowledge or satisfactory evidence of the identity of the individual requesting the protest.

167.71. Certificate of notarial act
(a) "**Commonwealth of Pennsylvania" may be used in lieu of "State of Pennsylvania" on certificates of notarial acts**.

(b) Sufficiency of certificate. A certificate must contain the information required by section 315(c) of the Act. A certificate may contain such other information as may be required to satisfy any legal requirements, or to satisfy ethical or legal concerns, or the business needs of the parties to the transaction.

(c) Securely attached. For purposes of attaching a notarial certificate to a tangible record, securely attached means stapled, grommeted or otherwise bound to the tangible record. Securely attached does not include the use of tape, paperclips or binder clips.

(d) When signing a paper certificate, the notary public shall use a legible, recognizable handwritten signature, which can be attributed to the notary performing the notarial act by anyone examining or authenticating the signature. If a notary's preferred signature is not legible and recognizable, the notary must also legibly print his or her name immediately adjacent to his or her preferred signature. For the purposes of this subsection, a signature is legible and recognizable if it is distinct, easily readable and understandable, and the notary's full name may be clearly discerned by looking at the signature.

Subchapter H. Use of Electronic Notarization
167.81. Notification regarding use of electronic notarization
(a) A notary public who wishes to perform notarial acts with respect to electronic records must hold a current and unrestricted commission.

(b) A notary public who wishes to perform notarial acts with respect to electronic records shall be authorized by the Department to act as an "electronic notary" or "e-notary" prior to performing notarial acts with respect to electronic records.

(c) To obtain authorization, a notary public shall submit the following information to the Department in a manner prescribed by the Department:

(1) Name of notary public
(2) Commission number
(3) Office address
(4) Email address
(5) Name of electronic notarization solution provider
(6) Contact information for solution provider
(7) Website for solution provider

167.82. Electronic notarization requirements
(a) A notary public performing notarial acts with respect to electronic records must use an electronic notarization solution approved by the Department. Before performing any electronic notarization, the notary shall take reasonable steps to ensure that the solution used is valid and has not expired, been revoked, or been terminated by the solution provider.

(b) All requirements of a notarial act performed with respect to a tangible record apply to an electronic record, including but not limited to, the personal appearance and identification of the individual appearing before the notary public, completion of a notarial certificate, use of an official stamp and recording of the notarial act in the notary journal.

167.111. Notary Public Examination.
(a) Pursuant to section 322(a) of the Revised Uniform Law on Notarial Acts (57 Pa.C.S. §322(a)), an applicant for a commission as a notary public who does not hold a commission in this Commonwealth must pass an examination as a condition of appointment. An applicant who does not hold a current commission as a notary public includes an applicant who never held a commission as a notary public and an applicant who previously held a commission as a notary public but whose commission has since expired.

(b) The written examination prescribed by the Department of State to determine the fitness of an applicant to exercise the functions of the office of notary public shall be a proctored examination administered by the Department of State or an agent of the Department. The
examination is administered by a professional testing organization under contract with the Department at times, places and costs established by the professional testing organization.

(c) Examination results shall be valid for a period of one (1) year from the date of the examination.

(d) An applicant must score 80% or better to pass the examination.

(e) An applicant may retake the examination within a six-month period as many times as necessary to pass. The maximum frequency with which the examination may be repeated is one time per 24-hour period.

(f) More information about the examination is available through the Department's website at www.dos.pa.gov/OtherServices/Notaries

167.124. Conduct providing the basis for disciplinary action.

(a) In addition to the acts and omissions specified by section 323(a) of the Act, the following acts or omissions demonstrate that an individual lacks the honesty, integrity, competence or reliability to act as a notary public:
(1) Notarizing his or her own signature or statement or a spouse's signature or statement.
(2) Notarizing records in blank.
(3) Post-dating or pre-dating notarial acts.
(4) Altering a document after it has been notarized.
(5) Issuing to the order of any State agency or the Commonwealth a personal check without sufficient funds on deposit.
(6) Performing a notarial act within the Commonwealth when the person was not commissioned as a notary public or was otherwise not authorized to perform a notarial act.
(7) Performing a notarial act in another state pursuant to the authority of the notary public's Pennsylvania commission.
(8) Making a representation that the notary public has powers, qualifications, rights or privileges that the notary public does not have.
(9) Use of the term "notario," "notario publico," "notario publica" or any non-English equivalent term in a manner which misrepresents the authority of the notary public.
(10) Engaging in the unauthorized practice of any regulated profession, including but not limited to law.

(11) Endorsing or promoting a product, service, contest or other offering by using the notary public's title or official stamp.
(12) Failure to require the physical presence of an individual making a statement in or executing a signature on a record.
(13) Failure to have personal knowledge or satisfactory evidence of the identity of an individual appearing before the notary.
(14) Executing a notarial certificate that contains a statement known to the notary public to be false.
(15) Using the notary public's official stamp for a purpose other than to perform a notarial act.
(16) Relating to commercial protests as defined in 13 Pa.C.S Section 3505(b), failure to identify the negotiable instrument, certify either that presentment has been made or, if not made, the reason why it was not made, and certify that the instrument has been dishonored by nonacceptance or nonpayment, or any combination of the above.
(17) Issuance of a certificate of dishonor of a negotiable instrument (also known as a protest of commercial paper as defined in 13 Pa.C.S. §3505(b)) that was owned or held for collection by a financial institution, trust company or investment company when the notary public was a party to the commercial paper in an individual capacity.
(18) Issuance of a certificate of dishonor of a negotiable instrument (also known as a protest of commercial paper as defined in 13 Pa.C.S. §3505(b)) of a non-commercial or other record that does not fit the definition of negotiable instrument as defined in 13 Pa.C.S. §3104.
(19) Issuance of a certificate of dishonor of a negotiable instrument (also known as a protest of commercial paper as defined in 13 Pa.C.S. §3505(b)) in a manner not in accordance with 13 Pa.C.S. §3505.
(20) Submission of the following types of records to the Department of State or Secretary of the Commonwealth in reply to correspondence from the Department or other government agency or initiating proceedings through the following record types:

(A) Conditional Acceptance, or a similar record purporting to "conditionally accept" presentment of an official record, and demanding proof of a list of claims in order to fully accept the official record.

(B) Affidavit in Support of Conditional Acceptance, or a similar record purporting to attest to the facts of a record and signed by the same notary public who is attesting.

(C) Notice of Dishonor, or a similar record purporting to give notice that a Conditional Acceptance has not been accepted by the government agency to which it was sent and thereby was dishonored.

(D) Accepted for Value, or similar stamp or certificate purporting to accept for a disclosed or undisclosed value an official record sent to the notary public by the Department of State, Secretary of the Commonwealth or other governmental agency. The certificate claims to establish an amount of money payable or accrued to the signor of the certificate.

(E) Notice of Protest, or a similar record purporting to be a Protest of Commercial Paper that has been dishonored, when said Commercial Paper is not, in fact, a negotiable instrument under Division 3 of Title 13 of the Pennsylvania Consolidated Statutes and subject to the laws stated therein regarding dishonor and protest.

(F) Other records attempting to apply Division 3 of Title 13 of the Pennsylvania Consolidated Statutes to non-negotiable instruments or other records not included in the scope of said chapter.

(G) Other record type purporting to follow the Uniform Commercial Code (UCC) and not related to a filing pursuant to Division 9 of Title 13 of the Pennsylvania Consolidated Statutes.

167.126. Unauthorized practice of law
(a) In determining whether a notary public has assisted a person in drafting legal records, gave legal advice or is otherwise practicing law (in violation of section 325 of the Act), the Department will take into consideration the factors in Pennsylvania Bar Association
Unauthorized Practice of Law (UPL) Committee Formal Opinion 2006-01 or any successor document to that opinion.

(b) Among the acts which constitute the practice of law are the preparation, drafting, or selection or determination of the kind of any legal document, or giving advice in relation to any legal documents or matters.

(c) No person who represents himself in a legal matter shall be considered to have engaged in the unauthorized practice of law.

167.127. Advertising
For the purpose of the statements required by section 325(d) of the Act (relating to representations), the term "prominently" in (d)(ii) means that the entire "I am not an attorney" statement must be in at least 10-point type and the term "prominently" in (d)(iii) means that the entire "I am not an attorney" statement must be displayed in an area open and accessible to the public at the place of performance of the notarial act.

LEGAL TERMS

The following are useful legal terms. They contain editorial comments intended to jump-start your understanding of the words. For official definitions, please consult a legal dictionary.

Acknowledgment – is a declaration that is made before an official (example: notary public) that under the person's free act and deed he did execute the instrument.

Administrator – An administrator of an estate is appointed by the court which empowers him to manage the affairs of the decedent (dead person).
The court appoints an administrator where a person dies without leaving a will, or leaves a will without naming an executor.

Affiant – An affidavit (a sworn to or affirmed written statement) is signed by a person called the affiant.

Affidavit – is a signed statement that is sworn to by the person signing it. An affidavit is sworn to in front of a notary public or other officer with authority to administer an oath.

Affirmation – A person who does not want to take an oath (because of religious, ethical or other reasons) may affirm as to the truthfulness of his statements. The act of affirming is called the affirmation. An affirmation is just as binding as an oath.

Apostile – An apostile is an authentication of a notarized document or other document. It is attached to the document and may be used internationally.

Attest – To attest is to be present at the execution of a written instrument and also to subscribe (sign) the written instrument as a witness to the execution of the instrument.

Attestation clause – As it refers to wills, an attestation clause is the written portion at the end of a will where the witnesses attest that the will was executed in front of them and also state the procedural manner of the execution of the will.

Chattel – Chattel means property that is personal in nature, such as household goods. Chattel does NOT include real property (land, buildings).

Chattel paper – A written obligation to pay money for specific goods is known as chattel paper

Cite – means to reference a legal authority, as to "cite" (refer to) a case.

Codicil – As it relates to wills, a codicil is an attachment to a will that adds to or changes (modifies) will in some way.

Commission – officially charged with a specific function.

Consideration – is what is given in value to induce someone to enter into a contract. Consideration examples are: property, money, services, etc.

Contempt of court – are actions which hinder the execution of court orders and display disrespect of court authority.

Contract – A contract (an agreement between parties) can be oral or written. For there to be a contract, there must be legal consideration to enter into the contract.

Conveyance – The instrument which creates, assigns, transfers or surrenders an interest in real property is called a conveyance.

Deponent – Deponent means the same as affiant. A deponent (affiant) is a person who signs the deposition and makes an oath to a written statement.

Deposition – A deposition is testimony taken before an authorized official (such as a notary public). It is taken out of court with the intention of using it at a hearing or trial.

Escrow – is depositing an instrument with a person who on the occurrence of an event must give the instrument to a designated person. Escrow is often used during the sale of a building.

Executor – is a person designated (named) in a will to carry out the instructions of the deceased that are listed in the will.

Ex Parte (one sided) – A court proceeding is ex parte (one sided) when it is conducted with only one of the parties being present (plaintiff or defendant).

Felony – Generally, a felony is an offense for which a sentence of imprisonment of more than a year may be imposed.

Guardian – A guardian is a person in charge of another person's property or person (usually relates to guardians of minors).

Judgment – A judgment declares the rights of individuals, including that one party owes money to another and specifying the amount owed. Judgments may be final or temporary.

Jurisdiction – refers to the extent of power to make decisions. For example: "The court has jurisdiction over that type of issue", or "The official has jurisdiction only within the county."

Lease – Lease is a contract regarding the right to the possession of real property (land or buildings). It is made for consideration (rent, lease payments) and transfers the right to possession of real property for a period of time.

Lien – A lien is the attachment of a legal claim on property until the debt on the property is satisfied.

Litigation – is the process of pursuing a lawsuit.

Misdemeanor – A crime that is not a felony. Misdemeanors are less serious than felonies and generally are punishable by a sentence of imprisonment up to and including a year.

Nolo contendere - acceptance of a plea of guilty without accepting guilt.

Oath – An oath or affirmation is a verbal pledge of the truthfulness of the statements made.

Plaintiff – A plaintiff is the party who starts a civil lawsuit.

Power of attorney – is a statement in writing by a person which gives another person the power to act for him.

Prima facie evidence - enough evidence to prove something, but which also can be refuted.

Proof – as it relates to the witnessing of the execution of instruments means the formal declaration of the witness that he witnessed the execution of the instrument. The witness must state his residence and that he knew the person signing the instrument.

Protest – written statement by a notary that a promissory note or bill of exchange was presented for acceptance or payment was refused.

Prothonotary – elected official in the Commonwealth of Pennsylvania.

Signature of notary public – Notary must sign his name (same name as under which appointed).

Statute – is a law that was created by the legislature.

Statute of frauds – A law that states that certain contracts must be in writing to be enforceable. Other contracts (if partially completed) may also be enforceable.

Statute of limitations - law which prescribe the time during which a civil action or criminal prosecution must be commenced.

Surety - money or property that is deposited to secure that a duty will be performed.

Swear – any mode of oath administration that is authorized by law.

Venue – is the geographical area where the affidavit or acknowledgment is taken by notary (Example: County of Albany).

Will – the instrument in which a person sets forth his wishes relating to the disposition of his property after his death.

FEES
(RULONA 329.1 and http://www.dos.pa.gov)
(Fees are set by the Department of State)

Notarial Service	Fee
Taking acknowledgment	$ 5
Taking acknowledgment (each additional name)	$ 2
Administering oath or affirmation (per individual taking oath or affirmation)	$ 5
Taking verification on oath or affirmation (no matter how many signatures)	$ 5
Witnessing or attesting a signature (per signature)	$ 5
Certifying or attesting a copy or deposition (per certified copy)	$ 5
Noting a protest of a negotiable instrument (per page)	$ 3

- Notaries may charge fees as set by Department of State.
- Fees must be separately stated.
- Fees may be waived by notaries.
- List of Fees must be displayed (if notary charges fees). In the alternative, notary may provide a list of fees to person requesting it.
- Fees are the property of the notary (and not the employer) unless the notary and employer enter into a different agreement.
- Notaries may charge clerical and administrative fees and customers should be informed prior to notarization.

A notary public may not charge any fee for notarizing the supporting affidavit required:
        1. in an Emergency Absentee Ballot, or
        2. the affidavit of a person needing assistance to vote an absentee ballot.

Also by the author of this book:

PENNSYLVANIA NOTARY PUBLIC JOURNAL

Large Entries

Property Of:
From __/__/__ to __/__/__

Large sized (8X10) and <u>value priced</u> notary public journal with 250 conveniently pre-formatted large entries, with space for all important notarial information.

QUICK QUESTIONS

Notary Public Law: Section 2
The Secretary of the Commonwealth is authorized to appoint and commission notaries public for a term of _____ years from the date of appointment.

Notary Public Law: Section 2
The jurisdiction of notaries public is coextensive with the boundaries of the _____.

Notary Public Law: Section 3
Any person who is ___ years of age or over, who resides or is employed within this Commonwealth and who is of good character, integrity and ability shall be eligible for the office of notary public.

Notary Public Law: Section 3
Any person who is a notary public and who resides outside this Commonwealth shall be deemed to have irrevocably appointed the _____ as the person's agent upon whom may be served any summons, subpoena, order or other process.

Notary Public Law: Section 5
Applications for appointment to the office of notary public shall be made to the _____.

ANSWERS

four

The Secretary of the Commonwealth is authorized to appoint and commission notaries public for a term of **four** years from the date of appointment.

Commonwealth

The jurisdiction of notaries public is coextensive with the boundaries of the **Commonwealth**.

18

Any person who is eighteen **(18)** years of age or over, who resides or is employed within this Commonwealth and who is of good character, integrity and ability shall be eligible for the office of notary public.

Notary Public Law: Section 3
Any person who is a notary public and who resides outside this Commonwealth shall be deemed to have irrevocably appointed the **Secretary of the Commonwealth** as the person's agent upon whom may be served any summons, subpoena, order or other process.

Secretary of the Commonwealth

Applications for appointment to the office of notary public shall be made to the **Secretary of the Commonwealth.**

QUICK QUESTIONS

Notary Public Law: Section 5
An applicant for notary public shall not have been convicted of or pled guilty or "nolo contendere" to a felony or a lesser offense incompatible with the duties of a notary public during the ____ year period preceding the date of the application.

Notary Public Law: Section 5
A notary applicant must complete at least ____ hours of approved notary education within the ____ month period immediately preceding his application.

Notary Public Law: Section 6
Application for Reappointment. Applications for reappointment to the office of notary public shall be filed at least ____ months prior to the expiration of the commission under which the notary is acting.

Notary Public Law: Section 7
If the notary changes his office address within the Commonwealth, notice in writing or electronically shall be given to the Secretary and the recorder of deeds of the county of original appointment by the notary within ____ days of such change.

Notary Public Law: Section 7
A notary public vacates his office by removing the notary's residence and _____ address from the Commonwealth, and such removal shall constitute a resignation from the office of notary public as of the date of removal.

ANSWERS

5

An applicant for notary public shall not have been convicted of or pled guilty or "nolo contendere" to a felony or a lesser offense incompatible with the duties of a notary public during the **5**-year period preceding the date of the application.

3....6

A notary applicant must complete at least three **3** hours of approved notary education within the **6**-month period immediately preceding his application.

2

Application for Reappointment. Applications for reappointment to the office of notary public shall be filed at least **2** months prior to the expiration of the commission under which the notary is acting.

5

If the notary changes his office address within the Commonwealth, notice in writing or electronically shall be given to the Secretary and the recorder of deeds of the county of original appointment by the notary within **5** days of such change.

business

A notary public vacates his office by removing the notary's residence and **business** address from the Commonwealth, and such removal shall constitute a resignation from the office of notary public as of the date of removal.

QUICK QUESTIONS

Notary Public Law: Section 8
Every notary, upon appointment and prior to entering the duties of notary public, shall take and subscribe the constitutional oath of office, and shall give a surety bond, payable to the Commonwealth of Pennsylvania, in the amount of $_____.

Notary Public Law: Section 8
Every notary bond shall have as surety a duly authorized surety company or ____ sufficient individual sureties, to be approved by the Secretary of the Commonwealth, conditioned for the faithful performance of the duties of the office of notary public.

Notary Public Law: Section 8
The notary bond ensures the faithful performance of the notary's duties and the delivery of notary's register and seal to the office of the recorder of deeds of the proper county in case of the death, resignation or disqualification of the notary within ____ days of such event.

Notary Public Law: Section 8
The notary public bond, as well as the commission and oath of office, shall be recorded in the _____ of the county in which the notary maintains an office at the time of appointment or reappointment.

Notary Public Law: Section 8
If a notary public fails to give bond and cause the bond and the commission and oath to be recorded within ____ days after the beginning of the term, his commission shall be null and void.

ACE THE PENNSYLVANIA NOTARY PUBLIC EXAM

ANSWERS

$10,000
Every notary, upon appointment and prior to entering the duties of notary public, shall take and subscribe the constitutional oath of office, and shall give a surety bond, payable to the Commonwealth of Pennsylvania, in the amount of **ten thousand dollars ($ 10,000)**.

two
Every notary bond shall have as surety a duly authorized surety company or **two** sufficient individual sureties, to be approved by the Secretary of the Commonwealth, conditioned for the faithful performance of the duties of the office of notary public.

30
The notary bond ensures the faithful performance of the notary's duties and the delivery of notary's register and seal to the office of the recorder of deeds of the proper county in case of the death, resignation or disqualification of the notary within thirty **(30)** days of such event.

office of the recorder of deeds
The notary public bond, as well as the commission and oath of office, shall be recorded in the **office of the recorder of deeds** of the county in which the notary maintains an office at the time of appointment or reappointment.

45
If a notary public fails to give bond and cause the bond and the commission and oath to be recorded within **(45)** days after the beginning of the term, his commission shall be null and void.

QUICK QUESTIONS

Notary Public Law: Section 9
The official notary signature shall be registered, in the "Notary Register" in the prothonotary's office of county where the notary maintains an office, within _____ days after appointment or reappointment.

Notary Public Law: Section 9
If a notary moves his office to another county, he must within _____ days thereafter register his signature in the prothonotary's office of county where the notary maintains an office.

Notary Public Law: Section 9
In acting as a notary public, a notary shall sign the notary's name exactly and only as it appears on the _____ or otherwise execute the notary's electronic signature in a manner that attributes such signature to the notary public identified on the commission.

Notary Public Law: Section 10
Change of Name. Whenever the name of any notary is changed by decree of court, or otherwise, such notary may continue to perform official acts, in the name in which he was commissioned, until the _____.

Notary Public Law: Section 10
When a notary changes his name, he must within thirty (30) days after entry of a name change decree, or after such name change, if not by decree of court, notify the _____ of such name change.

ANSWERS

45
The official notary signature shall be registered, in the "Notary Register" in the prothonotary's office of county where the notary maintains an office, within **45** days after appointment or reappointment. (In counties of the second class, such signature shall also be registered in the clerk of courts' office within said period.)

30
If a notary moves his office to another county, he must within **30** days thereafter register his signature in the prothonotary's office of county where the notary maintains an office. (In counties of the second class, such signature shall also be registered in the clerk of courts' office within said period.)

commission
In acting as a notary public, a notary shall sign the notary's name exactly and only as it appears on the **commission** or otherwise execute the notary's electronic signature in a manner that attributes such signature to the notary public identified on the commission.

expiration of his term
Change of Name. Whenever the name of any notary is changed by decree of court, or otherwise, such notary may continue to perform official acts, in the name in which he was commissioned, until the **expiration of his term.**

Secretary of the Commonwealth and recorder of deeds of county where he maintains an office
When a notary changes his name, he must within thirty (30) days after entry of a name change decree, or after such name change, if not by decree of court, notify the **Secretary of the Commonwealth and recorder of deeds of county where he maintains an office** of such name change.

QUICK QUESTIONS

Notary Public Law: Section 12
When certifying a copy of a document or other item, what must a notary public do?

Notary Public Law: Section 22.1
If an application or renewal is rejected, or a commission is revoked or recalled, or if a notary public resigns, applicant or notary shall deliver the seal to the Department of State within _____ days after notice from the department or from date of resignation, as the case may be.

Notary Public Law: Section 22.1 (Surrender of Seal)
Any person who violates the provisions of this subsection shall be guilty of a summary offense and upon conviction thereof shall be sentenced to pay a fine not exceeding $_____ or to imprisonment not exceeding _____ days, or both.

RULONA 304

A notarial officer (may / may not) perform a notarial act with respect to a record in which the notarial officer or the notarial officer's spouse has a direct or pecuniary interest.

RULONA 305
Notarial officer who takes an acknowledgment of a record shall determine, from _____ or satisfactory evidence of the identity of the person, that the Person appearing before notarial officer and making the acknowledgment is the person claimed.

ANSWERS

When certifying a copy of a document or other item, a notary public shall determine that the proffered copy is a full, true and accurate transcription or reproduction of that which was copied.

If an application or renewal is rejected, or a commission is revoked or recalled, or if a notary public resigns, applicant or notary shall deliver the seal to the Department of State within **ten (10)** days after notice from the department or from date of resignation, as the case may be.

Any person who violates the provisions of this subsection shall be guilty of a summary offense and upon conviction thereof shall be sentenced to pay a fine not exceeding **three hundred dollars ($ 300)** or to imprisonment not exceeding **ninety (90) days**, or both.

may not

A notarial officer **may not** perform a notarial act with respect to a record in which the notarial officer or the notarial officer's spouse has a direct or pecuniary interest.

Notarial officer who takes an acknowledgment of a record shall determine, from **personal knowledge** or satisfactory evidence of the identity of the person, that the Person appearing before notarial officer and making the acknowledgment is the person claimed.

QUICK QUESTIONS

RULONA 301

RULONA is the abbreviation for _____.

RULONA 302
"_____" is a declaration made in front of a notary that:
  (1) the person signed the record for the reason stated in the record; and that
  (2) if the person signed as a representative, he did so with proper authority.

RULONA 302

T/F? The definition for "Conviction" does not have to include a sentence ordered by the court.

RULONA 302

An electronic symbol, sound or process attached to or logically associated with a record and executed or adopted by an individual with the intent to sign the record is known as _____.

RULONA 302

T/F? A signature does not have to be in written form.

ANSWERS

RULONA is the abbreviation for
"Revised Uniform Law on Notarial Acts"

"**Acknowledgment**" is a declaration made in front of a notary that:
  (1) the person signed the record for the reason stated in the record; and that
  (2) if the person signed as a representative, he did so with proper authority.

True
"**Conviction**" means any of the following, even if a sentence was not ordered by a court:
  (1) An entry of a plea of guilty or "no contest".
  (2) A guilty verdict in a trial (with or without a jury).
  (3) Not guilty due to insanity, or guilty but mentally ill.

---

electronic signature
An electronic symbol, sound or process attached to or logically associated with a record and executed or adopted by an individual with the intent to sign the record is known as an **electronic signature**.

True
"Signature." can be a tangible symbol or an electronic signature which evidences the signing of a record.

QUICK QUESTIONS

RULONA 302

T/F? A stamping device can be physical or electronic.

RULONA 302

"_____" is a declaration made by an individual on oath or affirmation before a notarial officer, that a statement in a record is true. The term includes an affidavit.

RULONA 304
A notarial officer (may/may not) perform a notarial act with respect to a record in which the notarial officer or notarial officer's spouse has a direct or pecuniary interest.

RULONA 304
If a notary public performs a notarial act in which he has a pecuniary interest in the transaction, the notarial act is _____.

RULONA 305
A notarial officer who takes a verification of a statement on oath or affirmation shall determine identity from personal knowledge or _____ of the identity of the person.

ANSWERS

True

"Stamping device." Any of the following:
 (1) A physical device capable of affixing to or embossing on a tangible record an official stamp.
 (2) An electronic device or process capable of attaching to or logically associating with an electronic record an official stamp.

"**Verification on oath or affirmation**"

"**Verification on oath or affirmation**" is a declaration, made by an individual on oath or affirmation before a notarial officer, that a statement in a record is true. The term includes an affidavit.

may not

A notarial officer **may not** perform a notarial act with respect to a record in which the notarial officer or notarial officer's spouse has a direct or pecuniary interest.

voidable

If a notary public performs a notarial act in which he has a pecuniary interest in the transaction, the notarial act is **voidable**.

satisfactory evidence

A notarial officer who takes a verification of a statement on oath or affirmation shall determine identity from personal knowledge or **satisfactory evidence** of the identity of the person.

QUICK QUESTIONS

RULONA 306
If a notarial act relates to a statement made in or a signature executed on a record, person making statement or executing signature shall appear _____ before the notary.

RULONA 307
T/F? Satisfactory evidence of identity includes verification on oath or affirmation of a credible witness personally appearing before the notarial officer.

RULONA 308
Before a notary performs a notarial act, the notary must be satisfied that the individual executing the record is competent or has the capacity to execute the record.

RULONA 310
The signature and title of a notarial officer (does / does not) establish the authority of the notarial officer to perform the notarial act.

RULONA 310
Signature and title of an individual performing a notarial act in this Commonwealth are prima facie evidence that: (1) signature is genuine; and (2) _____.

ANSWERS

personally

If a notarial act relates to a statement made in or a signature executed on a record, person making statement or executing signature shall appear **personally** before the notary.

False

Satisfactory evidence of identity includes verification on oath or affirmation of a credible witness personally appearing before the notarial officer **and personally known to the notarial officer**.

True

The notary must also be satisfied that the individual's signature is knowingly and voluntarily made.

does

The signature and title of a notarial officer **does** establish the authority of the notarial officer to perform the notarial act.

individual holds designated title.

Signature and title of an individual performing a notarial act in this Commonwealth are prima facie evidence that: (1) signature is genuine; and (2) **individual holds designated title.**

QUICK QUESTIONS

RULONA 311
Does a notarial act performed in another state have the same effect under the law of this Commonwealth?

RULONA 312
Does a notarial act performed under the authority of a federally recognized Indian tribe have the same effect under the law of this Commonwealth?

RULONA 313
Does a notarial act performed under Federal authority have the same effect under the law of this Commonwealth?

RULONA 314
Does a notarial act performed under the authority of a foreign state have the same effect under the law of this Commonwealth?

RULONA 315
A notarial act shall be evidenced by a _____.

ANSWERS

Yes. Generally, it has the same effect
A notarial act performed in another state has the same effect under the law of this Commonwealth as if performed by a notarial officer of this Commonwealth if the act performed in that state is performed by a notary of that state, judge, clerk or other authorized individual.

Yes. Generally, it has the same effect
A notarial act performed under the authority of a federally recognized Indian tribe has the same effect under the law of this Commonwealth as if performed by a notarial officer of this Commonwealth if the act was performed by a notary, judge, clerk or other authorized individual of tribe.

Yes. Generally, it has the same effect
A notarial act performed under Federal authority has the same effect under the law of this Commonwealth as if performed by a notarial officer of this Commonwealth if the act was performed by a notary, judge, clerk or other Federally authorized individual.

Yes.
Also, a notarial act performed under the authority of a multinational or international governmental organization has the same effect under the law of this Commonwealth. This applies also to the Hague Convention and Consular authentications.

certificate
A notarial act shall be evidenced by a **certificate**.

QUICK QUESTIONS

RULONA 315
T?F? A notarial certificate does not have to be executed contemporaneously with the performance of the notarial act.

RULONA 315
A notarial certificate must be signed and _____ by the notarial officer.

RULONA 315
A notarial certificate must identify the county and _____ in which the notarial act is performed.

RULONA 315
A notarial certificate must contain the _____ of the notarial officer.

RULONA 315
The certificate of a notary must indicate the date of _____ of the notarial officer's commission.

ANSWERS

False

A notarial certificate MUST be executed contemporaneously with the performance of the notarial act.

dated

A notarial certificate must be signed and **dated** by the notarial officer.

state

A notarial certificate must identify the county and **State** in which the notarial act is performed. (Note also RULONA Regulations 167.71: State of Pennsylvania OR Commonwealth of Pennsylvania may be used.)

title

A notarial certificate must contain the **title** of the notarial officer.

expiration

The certificate of a notary must indicate the date of **expiration** of the notarial officer's commission.

QUICK QUESTIONS

RULONA 315
If a notarial act regarding a tangible record is performed by a notary public, an official stamp (may / shall) be affixed to the certificate.

RULONA 315
If a notarial act regarding a tangible record is performed by other than a notary public, an official stamp (may / shall) be affixed to the certificate.

RULONA 315
If a notarial act regarding an electronic record is performed by a notary public or other than a notary public, an official stamp (may / shall) be attached to or logically associated with the certificate.

RULONA 315
A notarial officer (may / may not) affix the notarial officer's signature to or logically associate it with a certificate until the notarial act has been performed.

RULONA 315
If a notarial act is performed regarding a tangible record, does a certificate have to be a part of or attached to the record?

ANSWERS

shall

If a notarial act regarding a tangible record is performed by a notary public, an official stamp **shall** be affixed to the certificate.

may

If a notarial act regarding a tangible record is performed by a notary public, an official stamp **may** be affixed to the certificate.

may

If a notarial act regarding an electronic record is performed by a notary public or other than a notary public, an official stamp **may** be attached to or logically associated with the certificate.

may not

A notarial officer **may not** affix the notarial officer's signature to or logically associate it with a certificate until the notarial act has been performed.

Yes

If a notarial act is performed regarding a tangible record, a certificate shall be part of or securely attached to the record. If a notarial act is performed regarding an electronic record, the certificate shall be affixed to or logically associated with the electronic record.

QUICK QUESTIONS

---

http://www.dos.pa.gov
The Revised Uniform Law on Notarial Acts (RULONA) requires that a notarial act must be evidenced by a _____.

---

http://www.dos.pa.gov
T/F? It is never acceptable for a notary to place one's signature and seal on a document, without any notarial language.

RULONA 317
The seal (may / must) be capable of being copied together with the record to which it is affixed or attached or with which it is logically associated.

RULONA 318
Who is responsible for the security of the stamping device of the notary public?

RULONA 318
May a notary public allow a trusted friend to use the stamping device to perform a notarial act?

ANSWERS

certificate
The Revised Uniform Law on Notarial Acts (RULONA) requires that a notarial act must be evidenced by a **certificate**.

True
The notary public must include a statement indicating the type of notarial act performed, showing when, where and before whom the notarial act was completed. It is never acceptable to place only one's signature and seal on a document, without any notarial language.

must
The seal **must** be capable of being copied together with the record to which it is affixed or attached or with which it is logically associated.

notary public
The **notary public** is responsible for the security of the stamping device of the notary public

No
A notary public may not allow another individual to use the stamping device to perform a notarial act.

QUICK QUESTIONS

RULONA 318
On resignation of a notary public commission or on the expiration of the date set forth in the stamping device, the notary public shall disable the stamping device by destroying, defacing, damaging, erasing or securing it against use in a manner which renders it _____.

RULONA 318
An individual whose notary commission has been suspended or revoked shall surrender possession of the stamping device to the _____.

RULONA 319
A notary public shall maintain a journal in which the notary public records in _____ order all notarial acts that the notary public performs.

RULONA 319
A journal may be created on a tangible medium or in an _____ format.

RULONA 319
If the journal is maintained on a tangible medium, it shall be a bound register with _____ pages.

ANSWERS

unusable

On resignation of a notary public commission or on the expiration of the date set forth in the stamping device, the notary public shall disable the stamping device by destroying, defacing, damaging, erasing or securing it against use in a manner which renders it **unusable**.

department

An individual whose notary commission has been suspended or revoked shall surrender possession of the stamping device to the **department**.

chronological

A notary public shall maintain a journal in which the notary public records in **chronological** order all notarial acts that the notary public performs.

electronic

A journal may be created on a tangible medium or in an **electronic** format.

numbered

If the journal is maintained on a tangible medium, it shall be a bound register with **numbered** pages.

QUICK QUESTIONS

RULONA 319
On death or incompetency of a notary public, the personal representative or guardian shall deliver the notary journal within ___ days to the office of recorder of deeds in county where notary maintained his office.

RULONA 319
T/F? A journal and each public record of the notary public are exempt from execution.

RULONA 319
A notary public shall give a _____ copy of the journal to a person that applies for it.

RULONA 319
A journal (may / may not) be used by any person other than the notary public.

RULONA 319
A journal (may / may not) be surrendered to an employer of the notary public upon termination of employment.

ANSWERS

30

On death or incompetency of a notary public, the personal representative or guardian shall deliver the notary journal within **30** days to the office of recorder of deeds in county where notary maintained his office.

True

A journal and each public record of the notary public are exempt from execution. A journal is the exclusive property of the notary.

certified

A notary public shall give a **certified** copy of the journal to a person that applies for it.

may not

A journal **may not** be used by any person other than the notary public.

may not

A journal **may not** be surrendered to an employer of the notary public upon termination of employment.

QUICK QUESTIONS

RULONA 320
Before a notary performs the initial notarial act with respect to an electronic record, a notary public shall notify the _____ that the notary will be performing notarial acts with respect to electronic records and identify each technology the notary intends to use.

RULONA 321
An applicant for appointment and commission as a notary public must be at least _____ years of age.

RULONA 321
An applicant for appointment and commission as a notary public must be a citizen or _____ of the United States.

RULONA 321
An applicant for appointment and commission as a notary public must be a resident or have a place of employment in _____.

RULONA 321
An applicant for appointment and commission as a notary public must be able to read and write _____.

ANSWERS

department

Before a notary performs the initial notarial act with respect to an electronic record, a notary public shall notify the **department** that the notary will be performing notarial acts with respect to electronic records and identify each technology the notary intends to use.

18

An applicant for appointment and commission as a notary public must be at least **18** years of age.

permanent legal resident

An applicant for appointment and commission as a notary public must be a citizen or **permanent legal resident** of the United States.

this Commonwealth

An applicant for appointment and commission as a notary public must be a resident or have a place of employment in **this Commonwealth**.

English

An applicant for appointment and commission as a notary public must be able to read and write **English**.

QUICK QUESTIONS

RULONA 321
A notary public application must be accompanied by a nonrefundable fee of $____, payable to the Commonwealth of Pennsylvania. This amount shall include the application fee for notary public commission and fee for filing of the bond with the department.

RULONA 321
Within 45 days after appointment and before issuance of a commission as a notary public, the applicant must obtain a surety bond in the amount of $_____ or the amount set by regulation of the department.

RULONA 321
T/F? If a notary public violates law with respect to notaries public in this Commonwealth, the surety or issuing entity is liable under the bond.

RULONA 321
The surety or issuing entity must give ___ days' notice to the department before canceling the bond.

RULONA 321
A notary public may perform notarial acts in this Commonwealth only during the period in which a _____ is on file with the department.

ANSWERS

$42

A notary public application must be accompanied by a nonrefundable fee of **$42**, payable to the Commonwealth of Pennsylvania. This amount shall include the application fee for notary public commission and fee for filing of the bond with the department.

$10,000

Within 45 days after appointment and before issuance of a commission as a notary public, the applicant must obtain a surety bond in the amount of **$10,000** or the amount set by regulation of the department.

True

If a notary public violates law with respect to notaries public in this Commonwealth, the surety or issuing entity is liable under the bond.

30

The surety or issuing entity must give **30** days' notice to the department before canceling the bond.
Also, the surety or issuing entity shall notify the department not later than 30 days after making a payment to a claimant under the bond.

valid bond

A notary public may perform notarial acts in this Commonwealth only during the period in which a **valid bond** is on file with the department.

QUICK QUESTIONS

RULONA 321
The official signature of each notary public shall be registered, for a fee of 50¢, in the "Notary Register" provided for that purpose in the _____ office of the county where the notary public maintains an office.

RULONA 321
The official signature of each notary public shall be registered within: (i) ____ days after appointment or reappointment; and (ii) ____ days after moving to a different county.

RULONA 321
In a county of the second class, the official signature of each notary public shall be registered in the office of
_____.

RULONA 321
Upon appointment and prior to entering into the duties of a notary public, the bond, oath of office and commission must be recorded in the office of the recorder of deeds of the county in which the notary public _____.

RULONA 321
Within ___ days of recording the bond, oath of office and commission in the office of the recorder of deeds, a copy of the bond and oath of office must be filed with the department.

ANSWERS

prothonotary's
The official signature of each notary public shall be registered, for a fee of 50¢, in the "Notary Register" provided for that purpose in the **prothonotary's** office of the county where the notary public maintains an office.

45....30
The official signature of each notary public shall be registered within: (i) **45** days after appointment or reappointment; and (ii) **30** days after moving to a different county.

the clerk of courts
In a county of the second class, the official signature of each notary public shall be registered in the office of **the clerk of courts**.

maintains an office
Upon appointment and prior to entering into the duties of a notary public, the bond, oath of office and commission must be recorded in the office of the recorder of deeds of the county in which the notary public **maintains an office**.

90
Within **90** days of recording the bond, oath of office and commission in the office of the recorder of deeds, a copy of the bond and oath of office must be filed with the department.

QUICK QUESTIONS

RULONA 321
A commission to act as a notary public (does / does not) not provide a notary public any immunity or benefit conferred by law of this Commonwealth on public officials or employees.

RULONA 322
A notary public applicant must, within the ___-month period immediately preceding application, complete a course of at least ___ hours of notary public basic education approved by the department.

RULONA 323
T/F? The department may impose sanctions for failure to comply with RULONA.

RULONA 323
An act which may result in sanctions of a notary public include conviction of a _____.

RULONA 323
T/F? An act which may result in sanctions of a notary public include conviction of any offense.

ANSWERS

does not

A commission to act as a notary public **does not** provide a notary public any immunity or benefit conferred by law of this Commonwealth on public officials or employees.

6....3

A notary public applicant must, within the **6**-month period immediately preceding application, complete a course of at least **3** hours of notary public basic education approved by the department. (Also applies to a renewal application.)

True

The department may impose sanctions for failure to comply with RULONA. Sanctions include denial, refusal to renew, suspend, reprimand or impose a condition on a commission as notary public

felony

An act which may result in sanctions of a notary public include conviction of a **felony** (or acceptance of Accelerated Rehabilitative Disposition for a felony or an offense involving fraud, dishonesty or deceit.)

False

An act which may result in sanctions of a notary public include conviction of any felony or other specified offenses.

QUICK QUESTIONS

RULONA 323
T/F? The department may deny a notary public commission if the applicant was denied a notary public commission in another state.

RULONA 323
The department may impose an administrative penalty of up to $_____ on a notary public for each act or omission which constitutes a violation of RULONA.

RULONA 323
T/F? A person may seek and obtain civil remedies against notaries public.

RULONA 323
T/F? Pretending to be a notary or a notarial officer and performing any action in furtherance of such false pretense shall subject the person to the penalties set forth in 18 Pa.C.S. § 4913 (relating to impersonating a notary public or a holder of a professional or occupational license).

RULONA 324
The database of notaries public verifies the authority of a notary public and indicates whether a notary public has notified the department that the notary public will be performing notarial acts on _____ records.

ANSWERS

True

Also may be denied for refusal to renew, revocation, suspension or conditioning of a notary public commission in another state.

$1,000

The department may impose an administrative penalty of up to **$1,000** on a notary public for each act or omission which constitutes a violation of RULONA. (May also be imposed on any person who performs a notarial act without being properly appointed and commissioned.

True

A person may also seek criminal penalties.

True

18 Pa.C.S. § 4913: Generally, a misdemeanor of the first or second degree. It includes use of an official stamp by a person who is not a notary.

electronic

The database of notaries public verifies the authority of a notary public and indicates whether a notary public has notified the department that the notary public will be performing notarial acts on **electronic** records.

QUICK QUESTIONS

RULONA 325
A commission as a notary public (does / does not) authorize the notary public to assist persons in drafting legal records, give legal advice or otherwise practice law.

RULONA 325
A commission as a notary public (does / does not) authorize the notary to act as an immigration consultant or an expert on immigration matters.

RULONA 325
A commission as notary public (does / does not) authorize the notary to represent a person in a judicial or administrative proceeding relating to immigration to the United States, or United States citizenship.

RULONA 325
A notary public who is not an attorney (may / may not) use the term "notario" or "notario publico".

RULONA 325
T/F? A notary public may advertise that he offers notarial services.

ANSWERS

does not

A commission as a notary public **does not** not authorize the notary public to assist persons in drafting legal records, give legal advice or otherwise practice law.

does not

A commission as a notary public **does not** authorize the notary to act as an immigration consultant or an expert on immigration matters.

does not

A commission as notary public **does not** authorize the notary to represent a person in a judicial or administrative proceeding relating to immigration to the United States, or United States citizenship.

may not

A notary public who is not an attorney **may not** use the term "notario" or "notario publico".

True

A notary public **may** advertise that he offers notarial services. In such a case, the notary must include in the advertisement a required prescribed statement regarding the limits of the services and that the notary is not an attorney. (Does not apply to attorneys.)

QUICK QUESTIONS

RULONA 326
The failure of a notarial officer to perform a duty or meet a requirement specified in this chapter (does / does not) invalidate a notarial act performed by the notarial officer.

RULONA 327
The department (may / may not) promulgate rules to implement the RULONA.

RULONA 327
Who establishes the process for approving and accepting surety bonds under section 321(d) (relating to appointment and commission as notary)?

RULONA 327
T/F? The department provides for administration of the examination under section 322(a) (relating to examination, basic education and continuing education) and course of study under section 322(b).

RULONA 327
The department may require applicants for appointment and commission as notaries public to submit _____ history record information as provided in 18 Pa.C.S. Ch. 91.

ANSWERS

does not

The failure of a notarial officer to perform a duty or meet a requirement specified in this chapter **does not** invalidate a notarial act performed by the notarial officer.

may

The department **may** promulgate rules to implement the RULONA.

the department

The department establishes the process for approving and accepting surety bonds under section 321(d) (relating to appointment and commission as notary).

True

The department also requires applicants for appointment and commission as notaries public to submit criminal history record information as provided in 18 Pa.C.S. Ch. 91 (relating to criminal history record information) as a condition of employment.

criminal

The department may require applicants for appointment and commission as notaries public to submit **criminal** history record information as provided in 18 Pa.C.S. Ch. 91.

ACE THE PENNSYLVANIA NOTARY PUBLIC EXAM

QUICK QUESTIONS

NOTARIES PUBLIC (57 PA.C.S.) - OMNIBUS AMENDMENTS
Act of Jul. 9, 2014, P.L. 1035, No. 119 Cl. 57 Session of 2014 No. 2014-119

An application for a commission as a notary public shall be accompanied by a nonrefundable fee of $___ , payable to the Commonwealth of Pennsylvania (fee for notary public commission and fee for filing of bond with the department).

NOTARIES PUBLIC (57 PA.C.S.) - OMNIBUS AMENDMENTS
Act of Jul. 9, 2014, P.L. 1035, No. 119 Cl. 57 Session of 2014 No. 2014-119

Section 321: Within ___ days after appointment or reappointment, and prior to entering into the duties of a notary public, the bond, oath of office and commission must be recorded in the office of the recorder of deeds of the county in which the notary public maintains an office.

NOTARIES PUBLIC (57 PA.C.S.) - OMNIBUS AMENDMENTS
Act of Jul. 9, 2014, P.L. 1035, No. 119 Cl. 57 Session of 2014 No. 2014-119

Section 321: Within ___ days of recording of the bond, oath of office and commission, a copy of the bond and oath of office must be filed with the department.

Uniform Acknowledgment Act - Section 6

T/F? An acknowledgment of a married woman may be made in the same form as though she were unmarried.

Uniform Acknowledgment Act - Section 8

The certificate of the acknowledging officer shall be completed by his signature, his official seal, if he has one, the title of his office, and, if he is a notary public, the date his _____ expires.

205

ANSWERS

NOTARIES PUBLIC (57 PA.C.S.) - OMNIBUS AMENDMENTS
Act of Jul. 9, 2014, P.L. 1035, No. 119 Cl. 57 Session of 2014 No. 2014-119

An application for a commission as a notary public shall be accompanied by a nonrefundable fee of **$42**, payable to the Commonwealth of Pennsylvania (fee for notary public commission and fee for filing of bond with the department).

NOTARIES PUBLIC (57 PA.C.S.) - OMNIBUS AMENDMENTS
Act of Jul. 9, 2014, P.L. 1035, No. 119 Cl. 57 Session of 2014 No. 2014-119

Within **45** days after appointment or reappointment, and prior to entering into the duties of a notary public, the bond, oath of office and commission must be recorded in the office of the recorder of deeds of the county in which the notary public maintains an office.

NOTARIES PUBLIC (57 PA.C.S.) - OMNIBUS AMENDMENTS
Act of Jul. 9, 2014, P.L. 1035, No. 119 Cl. 57 Session of 2014 No. 2014-119

Within **90** days of recording of the bond, oath of office and commission, a copy of the bond and oath of office must be filed with the department.

True
Marriage status does not change the form of an acknowledgment.

---

commission
The certificate of the acknowledging officer shall be completed by his signature, his official seal, if he has one, the title of his office, and, if he is a notary public, the date his **commission** expires.

QUICK QUESTIONS

Uniform Acknowledgment Act - Section 9

T/F? If the acknowledgment is taken within this State, or if taken without this State by an officer of this State, or is made without the United States by an officer of the United States, no authentication shall be necessary.

Uniform Acknowledgment Act - Section 10.1

Persons serving with Armed Forces of the US or their dependents may acknowledge the same before any commissioned officer in active service of the armed forces of the US with the rank of _____ or higher.

http://www.dos.pa.gov

The fee for taking an acknowledgment is _____ .

http://www.dos.pa.gov

The fee for taking an acknowledgment (each additional name) is _____ .

http://www.dos.pa.gov

The fee for administering oath or affirmation (per individual taking oath or affirmation) is _____ .

ACE THE PENNSYLVANIA NOTARY PUBLIC EXAM

ANSWERS

True
If acknowledgment is taken outside Pennsylvania, but in the US, a territory or insular possession of the US, or the District of Columbia, no authentication is necessary if the official before whom the acknowledgment is taken affixes his official seal to the instrument so acknowledged.

Second Lieutenant
Persons serving with Armed Forces of the US or their dependents may acknowledge the same before any commissioned officer in active service of the armed forces of the US with the rank of **Second Lieutenant** or higher.

$ 5

The fee for taking an acknowledgment is **$ 5**.

$ 2

The fee for taking an acknowledgment (each additional name) is **$ 2**.

$ 5

The fee for administering oath or affirmation (per individual taking oath or affirmation) is **$ 5**.

ACE THE PENNSYLVANIA NOTARY PUBLIC EXAM

QUICK QUESTIONS

---

http://www.dos.pa.gov

The fee for taking verification on oath or affirmation (no matter how many signatures) is $____.

---

http://www.dos.pa.gov

The fee for witnessing or attesting a signature (per signature) is $____.

---

http://www.dos.pa.gov

The fee for certifying or attesting a copy or deposition (per certified copy) is $____.

---

http://www.dos.pa.gov

The fee for noting a protest of a negotiable instrument (per page) is $_____.

---

http://www.dos.pa.gov

Notaries may only charge fees as set by the _____.

ANSWERS

$ 5

The fee for taking verification on oath or affirmation (no matter how many signatures) is **$ 5**.

$ 5

The fee for witnessing or attesting a signature (per signature) is **$ 5**.

$ 5

The fee for certifying or attesting a copy or deposition (per certified copy) is **$ 5**.

$ 3

The fee for noting a protest of a negotiable instrument (per page) is **$ 3**.

Department of State.

Notaries may only charge fees as set by the **Department of State**.

QUICK QUESTIONS

http://www.dos.pa.gov

Fees must be _____ stated.

---

http://www.dos.pa.gov

List of Fees must be displayed (if notary charges fees). In the alternative, notary may _____ .

---

http://www.dos.pa.gov

T/F? Fees may be waived by notaries.

---

http://www.dos.pa.gov

Fees are the property of the _____ (and not the employer) unless the notary and employer enter into a different agreement.

---

http://www.dos.pa.gov

Notaries may charge clerical and administrative fees and customers should be informed _____ to notarization.

ANSWERS

separately

Fees must be **separately** stated.

---

provide a list of fees to person requesting it.

List of Fees must be displayed (if notary charges fees). In the alternative, notary may **provide a list of fees to person requesting it**.

True

Fees may be waived by notaries.

---

notary

Fees are the property of the **notary** (and not the employer) unless the notary and employer enter into a different agreement.

---

prior

Notaries may charge clerical and administrative fees and customers should be informed **prior** to notarization.

QUICK QUESTIONS

RULONA Regulations 161.2

A notary public (may / may not) charge any fee for notarizing the supporting affidavit required in an Emergency Absentee Ballot or the affidavit of a person needing assistance to vote an absentee ballot.

RULONA Regulations 167.11

If a notary applicant is not a resident of Pennsylvania, the applicant must have a place of employment or practice in _____.

RULONA Regulations 167.13

If a notary public neither resides nor works in the Commonwealth, he is deemed to have resigned from the office of notary public and must notify the Department within ___ days of the effective date of resignation.

RULONA Regulations 167.14 (d)

If an applicant's preferred signature is not legible and recognizable, what must the applicant do?

RULONA Regulations 167.18

Notary public must notify Department of State within ___ days of any change in the information on file with the Department.

ANSWERS

may not

A notary public **may not** charge any fee for notarizing the supporting affidavit required in an Emergency Absentee Ballot or the affidavit of a person needing assistance to vote an absentee ballot.

this Commonwealth

If a notary applicant is not a resident of Pennsylvania, the applicant must have a place of employment or practice in **this Commonwealth**. (A post office box number is not a sufficient address for Department of State records.)

30

If a notary public neither resides nor works in the Commonwealth, he is deemed to have resigned from the office of notary public and must notify the Department within **30** days of the effective date of resignation.

If an applicant's preferred signature is not legible and recognizable, **the applicant must also legibly print his or her name immediately adjacent to his or her preferred signature**.

30

Notary public must notify Department of State within **30** days of any change in the information on file with the Department.

QUICK QUESTIONS

RULONA Regulations 167.21

167.22 d) Notification of loss or theft of stamping device under section 318(b) shall be made in writing or electronically to the Department within ___ days after the date the notary public or personal representative or guardian discovers that the stamping device was lost, misplaced, stolen or is otherwise unavailable.

RULONA Regulations 167.21

A notary journal (may / may not) contain any personal financial or identification information about the notary's clients, such as complete Social Security numbers, complete drivers' license numbers or complete account numbers.

RULONA Regulations 167.21

If a fee is waived or not charged, the notary public shall indicate this fact in the journal entry, using _____.

RULONA Regulations 167.21

Each page of the notary journal shall be _____ numbered from the beginning to the end of the journal.

RULONA Regulations 167.41

T/F? Neither initials alone nor nicknames will be accepted on the application or as part of the signature required on a notarial act.

ACE THE PENNSYLVANIA NOTARY PUBLIC EXAM

ANSWERS

10

Notification of loss or theft of stamping device under section 318(b) shall be made in writing or electronically to the Department within **10** days after the date the notary public or personal representative or guardian discovers that the stamping device was lost, misplaced, stolen or is otherwise unavailable.

may not

A notary journal **may not** contain any personal financial or identification information about the notary's clients, such as complete Social Security numbers, complete drivers' license numbers or complete account numbers.

If a fee is waived or not charged, the notary public shall indicate this fact in the journal entry, using **"n/c" or "0" (zero) or a similar notation**.

consecutively

Each page of the notary journal shall be **consecutively** numbered from the beginning to the end of the journal.

True

Neither initials alone nor nicknames will be accepted on the application or as part of the signature required on a notarial act. Also, the name of a notary MAY include suffixes (Junior, Senior, etc.) but MAY NOT include prefixes such a "Doctor", "Reverend", etc.

QUICK QUESTIONS

RULONA Regulations 167.41

The certificate of notarial act must be worded and completed using only letters, characters and a language that are read, written and understood by _____.

RULONA Regulations 167.48
A notarial officer may perform a notarial act on a document that is a translation of a document if the person performing the translation signs a _____ stating that the translation is accurate and complete.

RULONA Regulations 167.50

A notary public (may / may not) perform a notarial act with respect to a record which is designed to provide information within blank spaces.

RULONA Regulations 167.61
T/F? A record may be signed in the notarial officer's presence or a record may be signed prior to the acknowledgment.

RULONA Regulations 167.71
T/F? For purposes of attaching a notarial certificate to a tangible record, securely attached means stapled, grommeted or otherwise bound to the tangible record.

ANSWERS

the notarial officer

The certificate of notarial act must be worded and completed using only letters, characters and a language that are read, written and understood by **the notarial officer**.

A notarial officer may perform a notarial act on a document that is a translation of a document if the person performing the translation signs a **verification on oath or affirmation** stating that the translation is accurate and complete.

may not

A notary public **may not** perform a notarial act with respect to a record which is designed to provide information within blank spaces.

True

A record may be signed in the notarial officer's presence or a record may be signed prior to the acknowledgment.

(A record may not be signed subsequent to an acknowledgment.)

True

For purposes of attaching a notarial certificate to a tangible record, securely attached means stapled, grommeted or otherwise bound to the tangible record.
(Securely attached does not include the use of tape, paperclips or binder clips.)

QUICK QUESTIONS

RULONA Regulations 167.81
A notary public who wishes to perform notarial acts with respect to electronic records shall be authorized by the _____ to act as an "electronic notary" or "e-notary" prior to performing notarial acts with respect to electronic records.

RULONA Regulations 167.82

T/F? All requirements of a notarial act performed with respect to a tangible record apply to an electronic record.

RULONA Regulations 167.65
TF? If a record is intended to be sent overseas and requires an apostille or certification from the U.S. Department of State or Pennsylvania Department of State, the record must be certified by office where original or official copy of record is maintained or by the public official who issued the record.

RULONA Regulations 167.124

T/F? A notary may not notarize his or her own signature or statement or a spouse's signature or statement, notarize records in blank, or post-date or pre-date notarial acts.

RULONA Regulations 167.126

T/F? No person who represents himself in a legal matter shall be considered to have engaged in the unauthorized practice of law.

ANSWERS

A notary public who wishes to perform notarial acts with respect to electronic records shall be authorized by the **Department** to act as an "electronic notary" or "e-notary" prior to performing notarial acts with respect to electronic records.

True
All requirements of a notarial act performed with respect to a tangible record apply to an electronic record. (This includes personal appearance and identification of the individual appearing before the notary public, completion of a notarial certificate, use of an official stamp and recording of the notarial act in the notary journal).

True
Examples include deeds, marriage records, court orders and corporate documents filed with a state office or state repository as the official record.

True
Also a notary may not alter a document after it has been notarized, fail to require physical presence of an individual, make a statement in or executing a signature on a record, or fail to have personal knowledge or satisfactory evidence of the identity of an individual appearing before the notary.

True
No person who represents himself in a legal matter shall be considered to have engaged in the unauthorized practice of law.

ACE THE PENNSYLVANIA NOTARY PUBLIC EXAM

MULTIPLE CHOICE QUESTIONS

Which of the following is not listed as a notarial act in RULONA 302?

A. taking an acknowledgment
B. administering an oath or affirmation
C. witnessing or attesting a signature
D. testifying on a civil jury

A "Person." (RULONA 302) does not include:

A. Any individual
B. A government or governmental subdivision, agency or instrumentality.
C. A trained pet.
D. Any other legal or commercial entity.

In which of the following cases is a notary prohibited from performing a notarial act? In all cases where:

A. notary is a shareholder of a publicly traded company that is a party to the transaction.
B. the notarial officer's wife has a pecuniary interest
C. notary is an employee of a corporate party
D. fee of notary is not contingent on the transaction

221

ANSWERS

D. testifying on a civil jury
(RULONA 302)

Other <u>valid</u> notarial acts include:
- taking a verification on oath or affirmation
- certifying or attesting a copy or deposition
- noting a protest of a negotiable instrument.

C. A trained pet
(RULONA 302)

"Person" also includes "corporation, business trust, statutory trust, estate, trust, partnership, limited liability company, association, joint venture or public corporation."

B. the notarial officer's wife has a pecuniary interest
(RULONA 304)

A notarial officer may not perform a notarial act with respect to a record in which the notarial officer or the notarial officer's spouse has a direct or pecuniary interest.

MULTIPLE CHOICE QUESTIONS

Specified satisfactory evidence includes all of the following, except:

A. a passport
B. a driver's license
C. nondriver identification card
D. an IRS W-2 form

If the notary determines that the individual's signature on the record or statement does not conform to the signature on a form of identification used to determine the identity of the individual; the notary public:
A. can accept either signature.
B. can charge a higher fee because of the default.
C. may not question the identity.
D. may refuse to perform the notarial act.

Which of the following is not correct? A notarial act may be performed in this Commonwealth by:
A. A judge of a court of record.
B. A clerk, deputy clerk of a court having a seal.
C. A recorder of deeds or deputy recorder of deeds.
D. Any pharmacist employed by a large chain.

ANSWERS

D. an IRS W-2 form
(RULONA 307)

Any government ID not specified in RULONA 307 must be: (A) is current; (B) contains the signature or a photograph of the individual; and (C) is satisfactory to the notarial officer.

D. may refuse to perform the notarial act
(RULONA 308)

A notarial officer **may refuse to perform a notarial act** if the notarial officer is not satisfied that the individual's signature on the record or statement substantially conforms to the signature on a form of identification used to determine the identity of the individual.

D. Any pharmacist employed by a large chain.
(RULONA 310)

(The pharmacist must be a commissioned notary public) A notarial act may also be performed by a prothonotary or deputy prothonotary (Chief Clerk and Deputy Chief Clerk involved with non-criminal court records such as property deeds and marriage licenses.)

MULTIPLE CHOICE QUESTIONS

Which of the following is not specifically authorized to perform notarial acts?

A. a notary public
B. a member of the major judiciary
C. certain clerks of recorder of deeds
D. an individual authorized by law

Which of the following is not correct? A notarial certificate:

A. must be executed contemporaneously with the performance of the notarial act.
B. be signed and dated by the notarial officer.
C. must state the country in which executed.
D. must contain the title of the notarial officer.

Which of the following is not a short form certificate of notarial action?

A. Verification on oath or affirmation
B. Witnessing or attesting a signature
C. Certifying a reconstructed record as a true copy.
D. Certifying the transcript of a deposition

ANSWERS

B. a member of the major judiciary
(RULONA 310)

The correct answer is: a member of the **minor** judiciary.

C. must state the country in which executed
(RULONA 315)

The notarial certificate must identify the **county and State** in which the notarial act is performed;

C. Certifying a reconstructed record as a true copy.
(RULONA 316)

This should read: "Certifying a **copy** of a record".
Other valid short form certificates are:
(1) Acknowledgment in an individual capacity
(2) Acknowledgment in a representative capacity
(3) Acknowledgment by an attorney at law

ACE THE PENNSYLVANIA NOTARY PUBLIC EXAM

MULTIPLE CHOICE QUESTIONS

Which of the following do not apply to the official stamp of a notary public?

A. The words "Commonwealth of Pennsylvania"
B. The words "Navy Seal".
C. County where notary public maintains his office.
D. Date notary public's commission expires.

Which of the following do not apply to the official stamp of a notary public?

A. The name as it appears on the commission of the notary public and the words "Notary Public."
B. The words "Notary Seal."
C. The date the notary public's commission expires.
D. The date of birth of the notary.

Which is not correct? A notary journal entry contains:

A. Date and time of notarial act
B. Description of record, if any, and type of notarial act.
C. Initials and address of each individual for whom notarial act is performed.
D. If identity of individual is based on personal knowledge, a statement to that effect.

ANSWERS

B. The words "Navy Seal"
(RULONA 317)

This should read, "**Notary** Seal".

D. The date of birth of the notary
(RULONA 317)

The date of birth of the notary is <u>not</u> a requirement on the official stamp.

C. Initials and address of each individual for whom notarial act is performed.
(RULONA 319)

This should read: The <u>full name</u> and address of each individual for whom notarial act is performed.

MULTIPLE CHOICE QUESTIONS

If a notary resigns or his commission is revoked, he shall deliver the journal of the notary public to the office of the recorder of deeds in the county where the notary public last maintained an office within ____ days of resignation or revocation of commission.
A. 10
B. 30
C. 45
D. 60

A notary public may advertise or represent that the notary public may:
A. assist persons in drafting legal records.
B. give legal advice.
C. practice law.
D. perform notarial duties

Which of the following is not correct? The acknowledgment of any instrument within this state may be made before:
A. judge of a court of record.
B. clerk, prothonotary or deputy prothonotary.
C. deputy clerk of a court having a seal.
D. a secretary of an attorney.

ANSWERS

B. 30
(RULONA 319)

If a notary resigns or his commission is revoked, he shall deliver the journal of the notary public to the office of the recorder of deeds in the county where the notary public last maintained an office within **30** days of resignation or revocation of commission.

D. perform notarial duties
(RULONA 325)

A notary public may not advertise or represent that the notary public may assist persons in drafting legal records, give legal advice or practice law.

D. a secretary of an attorney
(Uniform Acknowledgment Act - Section 2

A secretary of an attorney is not correct because the choice does not state that the secretary is a commissioned notary public.

MULTIPLE CHOICE QUESTIONS

Which of the following is not correct? The acknowledgment of any instrument within this state may be made before a:
A. recorder of deeds or deputy recorder of deeds
B. bank supervisor
C. notary public
D. justice of the peace, magistrate or alderman

Which of the following is not correct?
The acknowledgment of any instrument may be made without the State, but within the United States by:
A. a clerk or deputy of any federal court;
B. a federal employee in good standing
C. a clerk, prothonotary or deputy prothonotary or deputy clerk of any court of record of any state or other jurisdiction;
C. a notary public, a recorder of deeds.

Which of the following is not correct?
The acknowledgment of any instrument may be made outside the US before:
A. an ambassador, minister, charge d' affaires, consul, commercial attaché
B. a notary public of country where acknowledgment is made;
C. an official interpreter
D. a judge or clerk of a court of record of the country where acknowledgment is made.

231

ANSWERS

B. bank supervisor
(Uniform Acknowledgment Act - Section 2)

A bank supervisor is not correct because the choice does not state that the bank supervisor is a commissioned notary public.

B. a federal employee in good standing
(Uniform Acknowledgment Act - Section 3)

A "federal employee in good standing" is not correct because the choice does not state that the person is a commissioned notary public.

C. an official interpreter
(Uniform Acknowledgment Act - Section 4)

An official interpreter is not listed as an authorized official.

MULTIPLE CHOICE QUESTIONS

Which of the following is eligible to hold the office of notary public?

A. judge of a higher court.
B. member of Congress.
C. the head of a Pennsylvania state department
D. a druggist who qualifies for the office

The seal shall have a maximum height of _____, with a plain border.

A. (.5) inch and width of two and one-half (2 1/2)
B. (1.5) inch and width of three and one-half (3 1/2)
C. (1) inch and width of three and one-half (3 1/2)
D. (2) inch and width of four and one-half (4 1/2)

Which of the following is not correct?
A notary is not required to use an electronic seal, if the following information is attached to the electronic signature or electronic record being notarized, acknowledged or verified:
A. The full name of the notary along with the words "Notary Public."
B. The name of the county in which the notary maintains an office.
C. The date the notary's commission is due to expire.
D. The brand name of the electronic device being employed.

ANSWERS

D. a druggist who qualifies for the office
(Notary Public Law: Section 4)

(1) Any person holding any judicial office in this Commonwealth, except the office of justice of the peace, magistrate, or alderman.
(2) Every member of Congress, and any person, whether an officer, a subordinate officer, or agent, holding any office or appointment of profit or trust under the legislative, executive, or judiciary departments of the government of the United States, to which a salary, fees or perquisites are attached.

C. (1) inch and width of three and one-half (3 1/2)
(Notary Public Law: Section 12)

The seal shall be stamped in a prominent place on the official notarial certificate near the notary's signature in such a manner as to be capable of photographic reproduction.

D. The brand name of the electronic device being employed.
(Notary Public Law: Section 12)

ACE THE PENNSYLVANIA NOTARY PUBLIC EXAM

MULTIPLE CHOICE QUESTIONS

Which of the following is not correct?
Notaries have power to:

A. administer oaths
B. certify copies
C. take affidavits
D. interrogate witnesses during a trial

Which of the following is not correct?
Notaries have power to:

A. administer affirmations
B. take depositions
C. adjudge a person in contempt
D. take verifications

Which of the following regarding notary fees is not correct?
A. Fees of notaries shall be fixed by the Secretary with approval of the Attorney General.
B. A notary shall not charge a fee in excess of fees fixed by the Secretary.
C. Fees of notaries public shall be displayed in a conspicuous location in the notary's place of business or provided upon request to any person utilizing the services of the notary.
D. A notary may charge a greater fee for time-consuming cases.

ANSWERS

D. interrogate witnesses during a trial
(Notary Public Law: Section 16)

C. adjudge a person in contempt
(Notary Public Law: Section 16)

D. A notary may charge a greater fee for time-consuming cases.
(Notary Public Law: Section 21)

MULTIPLE CHOICE QUESTIONS

Which of the following regarding notary fees is not correct?

A. The fees of the notary shall be separately stated.
B. A notary public may waive the right to charge a fee, in which case the fees do not have to be displayed.
C. A notary fee charged by an attorney may be double the statutory fee.
D. The fee for any notary public employed by a bank or banking institution shall be the property of the notary.

The jurisdiction of notaries public is coextensive with the boundaries of the _____.

A. United States
B. North America
C. Commonwealth
D. county where principal office is located

Any person who is a notary public and who resides outside this Commonwealth shall be deemed to have irrevocably appointed the _____ as the person's agent upon whom may be served any summons, subpoena, order or other process.

A. clerk of the county
B. public attorney
C. Comptroller of the Commonwealth
D. Secretary of the Commonwealth

ANSWERS

C. A notary fee charged by an attorney may be double the statutory fee.
(Notary Public Law Section 21)

C. Commonwealth

The jurisdiction of notaries public is coextensive with the boundaries of the **Commonwealth**.

D. Secretary of the Commonwealth
(Notary Public Law: Section 3)

Any person who is a notary public and who resides outside this Commonwealth shall be deemed to have irrevocably appointed **Secretary of the Commonwealth** as the person's agent upon whom may be served any summons, subpoena, order or other process.

MULTIPLE CHOICE QUESTIONS

A notary applicant must complete at least ___ hours of approved notary education within the ___ month period immediately preceding their application.

A. 6....3
B. 3....3
C. 3...12
D. 3....6

An applicant for notary public shall not have been convicted of or pled guilty or "nolo contendere" to a _____ or a lesser offense incompatible with the duties of a notary public during the ____ year period preceding the date of the application.

A. offense....3
B. felony....5
C. misdemeanor....3
D. petty offense....5

Application for Reappointment to the office of notary public shall be filed at least ___ months prior to the expiration of the commission under which the notary is acting.

A. 2
B. 3
C. 4
D. 6

ACE THE PENNSYLVANIA NOTARY PUBLIC EXAM

ANSWERS

D. 3....6
(Notary Public Law: Section 5)

A notary applicant must complete at least **3** hours of approved notary education within the **6**-month period immediately preceding their application.

B. felony....5
(Notary Public Law: Section 5)

An applicant for notary public shall not have been convicted of or pled guilty or "nolo contendere" to a **felony** or a lesser offense incompatible with the duties of a notary public during the **5**-year period preceding the date of the application.

A. 2
(Notary Public Law: Section 6)

Application for Reappointment. to the office of notary public shall be filed at least **two** months prior to the expiration of the commission under which the notary is acting

ACE THE PENNSYLVANIA NOTARY PUBLIC EXAM

MULTIPLE CHOICE QUESTIONS

If the notary changes his office address within the Commonwealth, notice in writing or electronically shall be given to the Secretary and the recorder of deeds of the county of original appointment by the notary within ___ days of such change.

A. 5
B. 10
C. 20
D. 30

Every notary, upon appointment and prior to entering the duties of notary public, shall take and subscribe the constitutional oath of office, and shall give a surety bond, payable to the Commonwealth of Pennsylvania, in the amount of $_____.

A. $ 5,000
B. $ 10,000
C. $ 15,000
D. $ 20,000

The notary public bond, as well as the commission and oath of office, shall be recorded in the _____ of the county in which the notary maintains an office at the time of appointment or reappointment.
A. office of the chief clerk
B. comptroller's office
C. office of the recorder of deeds
D. fiduciary office

ANSWERS

A. 5
(Notary Public Law: Section 7)

If the notary changes his office address within the Commonwealth, notice in writing or electronically shall be given to the Secretary and the recorder of deeds of the county of original appointment by the notary within **5** days of such change.

B. $ 10,000
(Notary Public Law: Section 8)

Every notary, upon appointment and prior to entering the duties of notary public, shall take and subscribe the constitutional oath of office, and shall give a surety bond, payable to the Commonwealth of Pennsylvania, in the amount of **ten thousand dollars ($ 10,000)**.

C. office of the recorder of deeds
(Notary Public Law: Section 8)

The notary public bond, as well as the commission and oath of office, shall be recorded in the **office of the recorder of deeds** of the county in which the notary maintains an office at the time of appointment or reappointment.

MULTIPLE CHOICE QUESTIONS

If a notary public fails to give bond and cause the bond and the commission and oath to be recorded within ___ days after the beginning of the term, his commission shall be null and void.

A. 10
B. 15
C. 30
D. 45

The official notary signature shall be registered, in the "Notary Register" in the prothonotary's office of county where the notary maintains an office, within ___ days after appointment or reappointment.

A. 10
B. 15
C. 30
D. 45

If a notary moves his office to another county, he must within ___ days thereafter register his signature in the prothonotary's office of county where the notary maintains an office.

A. 10
B. 15
C. 20
D. 30

ANSWERS

D. 45
(Notary Public Law: Section 8)

If a notary public fails to give bond and cause the bond and the commission and oath to be recorded within **45** days after the beginning of the term, his commission shall be null and void.

D. 45
(Notary Public Law: Section 9)

The official notary signature shall be registered, in the "Notary Register" in the prothonotary's office of county where the notary maintains an office, within **45** days after appointment or reappointment. (In counties of the second class, such signature shall also be registered in the clerk of courts' office within said period.)

D. 30
(Notary Public Law: Section)

If a notary moves his office to another county, he must within **30** days thereafter register his signature in the prothonotary's office of county where the notary maintains an office. (In counties of the second class, such signature shall also be registered in the clerk of courts' office within said period.)

MULTIPLE CHOICE QUESTIONS

In acting as a notary public, a notary shall sign the notary's name exactly and only as it appears on the _____ or otherwise execute the notary's electronic signature in a manner that attributes such signature to the notary public identified on the commission.

A. birth certificate
B. social security card
C. notary public commission
D. graduation certificate

Whenever the name of any notary is changed by decree of court, or otherwise, such notary may continue to perform official acts, in the name in which he was commissioned, until _____.

A. the expiration of 10 days.
B. the expiration of 30 days.
C. the end of the calendar year.
D. the expiration of his term.

RULONA is the abbreviation for _____.

A. Redrafted Unaltered Law on Notarial Acts
B. Reviewed Unmodified Law on Notarial Acts
C. Reworked Uniform Law on Notarial Acts
D. Revised Uniform Law on Notarial Acts

ANSWERS

C. notary public commission
(Notary Public Law: Section 9)

In acting as a notary public, a notary shall sign the notary's name exactly and only as it appears on the **commission** or otherwise execute the notary's electronic signature in a manner that attributes such signature to the notary public identified on the commission.

D. the expiration of his term.
(Notary Public Law: Section 10)

Whenever the name of any notary is changed by decree of court, or otherwise, such notary may continue to perform official acts, in the name in which he was commissioned, until the **expiration of his term.**

D. Revised Uniform Law on Notarial Acts
(RULONA 301)

RULONA is the abbreviation for **Revised Uniform Law on Notarial Acts**.

MULTIPLE CHOICE QUESTIONS

"_____" is a declaration in front of a notary that:
(1) the person signed the record for the reason stated in the record; and that
(2) if the person signed as a representative, he did so with proper authority.

A. transfiguration
B. bonafied statement
C. acknowledgment
D. assessment

"_____" is a declaration made by an individual on oath or affirmation before a notarial officer, that a statement in a record is true. The term includes an affidavit.

A. statement
B. Verification on oath or affirmation
C. soliloquy
D. affirment

If a notary public performs a notarial act in which he has a pecuniary interest in the transaction, the notarial act is _____.

A. financially sound
B. monetarily recorded
C. permissible
D. voidable

ANSWERS

C. acknowledgment
(RULONA 302)

"**Acknowledgment**" is a declaration in front of a notary that:
(1) the person signed the record for the reason stated in the record; and that
(2) if the person signed as a representative, he did so with proper authority.

B. Verification on oath or affirmation
(RULONA 302)

"**Verification on oath or affirmation**" is a declaration, made by an individual on oath or affirmation before a notarial officer, that a statement in a record is true. The term includes an affidavit.

D. voidable
(RULONA 304)

If a notary public performs a notarial act in which he has a pecuniary interest in the transaction, the notarial act is **voidable**.

MULTIPLE CHOICE QUESTIONS

If a notarial act relates to a statement made in or a signature executed on a record, person making statement or executing signature shall appear _____ before the notary.

A. by telephone
B. text message
C. by video conference
D. personally

A notarial act shall be evidenced by a _____.

A. copy of the document.
B. transcript of judgment.
C. certificate.
D. certified copy of the ID.

A notarial certificate must be executed:

A. 24 hours before the acknowledgment.
B. contemporaneously with the performance of the notarial act.
C. in front of 2 witnesses.
D. with malintent.

ANSWERS

D. personally
(RULONA 306)

If a notarial act relates to a statement made in or a signature executed on a record, person making statement or executing signature shall appear **personally** before the notary.

C. certificate
(RULONA 315)

A notarial act shall be evidenced by a **certificate**.

B. contemporaneously with the performance of the notarial act.
(RULONA 315)

A notarial certificate must be executed **contemporaneously with the performance of the notarial act**.

MULTIPLE CHOICE QUESTIONS

A notarial certificate must identify the county and _____ in which the notarial act is performed.

A. town
B. village
C. city
D. state

The certificate of a notary must indicate the date of _____ of the notarial officer's commission.

A. commencement
B. anniversary
C. expiration
D. initiation

Who is responsible for the security of the stamping device of the notary public?

A. the county clerk
B. the register of deeds
C. the Secretary of the Commonwealth
D. the notary public

ACE THE PENNSYLVANIA NOTARY PUBLIC EXAM

ANSWERS

D. state
(RULONA 315)

A notarial certificate must identify the county and **State** in which the notarial act is performed.

C. expiration
(RULONA 315)

The certificate of a notary must indicate the date of **expiration** of the notarial officer's commission.

D. the notary public
(RULONA 318)

The **notary public** is responsible for the security of the stamping device of the notary public.

MULTIPLE CHOICE QUESTIONS

A notary public shall maintain a journal in which the notary public records in _____ order all notarial acts that the notary public performs.

A. lunar calendar
B. chronological
C. alphabetical
D. limit

If the journal is maintained on a tangible medium, it shall be a bound register with _____ pages.

A. 8.5 X 11 inches
B. numbered
C. more than 100
D. white

On death or incompetency of a notary public, the personal representative or guardian shall deliver the notary journal within ___ days to the office of recorder of deeds in county where notary maintained his office.

A. 30
B. 45
C. 60
D. 15

ANSWERS

B. chronological
(RULONA 319)

A notary public shall maintain a journal in which the notary public records in **chronological** order all notarial acts that the notary public performs.

B. numbered
(RULONA 319)

If the journal is maintained on a tangible medium, it shall be a bound register with **numbered** pages.

A. 30
(RULONA 319)

On death or incompetency of a notary public, the personal representative or guardian shall deliver the notary journal within **30** days to the office of recorder of deeds in county where notary maintained his office.

MULTIPLE CHOICE QUESTIONS

Before a notary performs the initial notarial act with respect to an electronic record, a notary public shall notify the _____ that the notary will be performing notarial acts with respect to electronic records and identify each technology the notary intends to use.
A. county clerk
B. chief clerk
C. county assessor
D. department

An applicant for appointment and commission as a notary public must be able to read and write _____.

A. Spanish and English
B. at least English and one other language
C. three languages
D. English

An applicant for appointment and commission as a notary public must be at least ____ years of age and be a citizen or _____ of the United States.

A. 21...foreign national
B. 18...permanent legal resident
C. 21...alien resident
D. 18...temporary resident

ANSWERS

D. department
(RULONA 320)

Before a notary performs the initial notarial act with respect to an electronic record, a notary public shall notify the **department** that the notary will be performing notarial acts with respect to electronic records and identify each technology the notary intends to use.

D. English
(RULONA 321)

An applicant for appointment and commission as a notary public must be able to read and write English.

B. 18...permanent resident
(RULONA 321)

An applicant for appointment and commission as a notary public must be at least **18** years of age and be a citizen or **permanent legal resident** of the United States.

MULTIPLE CHOICE QUESTIONS

An applicant for appointment and commission as a notary public must be a resident or have a place of employment in _____ and be able to read and write _____.

A. this Commonwealth...English
B. Pennsylvania...two languages
C. this Commonwealth...Spanish
D. the county of appointment...two languages

A notary public application must be accompanied by a nonrefundable fee of $____, payable to the Commonwealth of Pennsylvania. This amount shall include the application fee for notary public commission and fee for filing of the bond with the department.
A. $ 30
B. $ 42
C. $ 50
D. $ 65

The surety or issuing entity must give ___ days' notice to the department before canceling the notary bond.

A. 10
B. 15
C. 20
D. 30

ANSWERS

A. this Commonwealth...English
(RULONA 321)

An applicant for appointment and commission as a notary public must be a resident or have a place of employment in **this Commonwealth** and be able to read and write **English**.

B. $ 42
(RULONA 321)

A notary public application must be accompanied by a nonrefundable fee of **$42**, payable to the Commonwealth of Pennsylvania. This amount shall include the application fee for notary public commission and fee for filing of the bond with the department.

D. 30
(RULONA 321)

The surety or issuing entity must give **30** days' notice to the department before canceling the notary bond. Also, the surety or issuing entity shall notify the department not later than 30 days after making a payment to a claimant under the bond.

MULTIPLE CHOICE QUESTIONS

The official signature of each notary public shall be registered, for a fee of 50¢, in the "Notary Register" provided for that purpose in the _____ of the county where the notary public maintains an office.

A. fiscal office
B. monetary records
C. fees and registration
D. prothonotary's office

The official signature of each notary public shall be registered within: (i) ____ days after appointment or reappointment; and (ii) ____ days after moving to a different county.

A. 30...45
B. 30...60
C. 45...30
D. 45...60

Within ____ days of recording the bond, oath of office and commission in the office of the recorder of deeds, a copy of the bond and oath of office must be filed with the department.

A. 30
B. 60
C. 90
D. 15

ANSWERS

D. prothonotary's office
(RULONA 321)

The official signature of each notary public shall be registered, for a fee of 50¢, in the "Notary Register" provided for that purpose in the **prothonotary's** office of the county where the notary public maintains an office.

C. 45...30
(RULONA 321)

The official signature of each notary public shall be registered within: (i) **45** days after appointment or reappointment; and (ii) **30** days after moving to a different county.

C. 90
(RULONA 321)

Within **90** days of recording the bond, oath of office and commission in the office of the recorder of deeds, a copy of the bond and oath of office must be filed with the department.

MULTIPLE CHOICE QUESTIONS

The department may impose an administrative penalty of up to $_____ on a notary public for each act or omission which constitutes a violation of RULONA.

A. $ 250
B. $ 500
C. $ 750
D. $ 1,000

A notary public who is not an attorney may not use the terms _____ or _____.

A. notary public or notary
B. "notario" or "notario publico"
C. notary or notary public
D. none of the above

The department may require applicants for appointment and commission as notaries public to submit _____ history record information as provided in 18 Pa.C.S. Ch. 91.

A. criminal
B. tax
C. school
D. bank

ANSWERS

D. $ 1,000
(RULONA 323)

The department may impose an administrative penalty of up to **$1,000** on a notary public for each act or omission which constitutes a violation of RULONA. (May also be imposed on any person who performs a notarial act without being properly appointed and commissioned.)

B. "notario" or "notario publico"
(RULONA 325)

A notary public who is not an attorney **may not** use the term "notario" or "notario publico".

A. criminal
(RULONA 327)

The department may require applicants for appointment and commission as notaries public to submit **criminal** history record information as provided in 18 Pa.C.S. Ch. 91.

ACE THE PENNSYLVANIA NOTARY PUBLIC EXAM

MULTIPLE CHOICE QUESTIONS

---

www.dos.pa.gov

The fee for taking an acknowledgment is _____.:

A. $ 2
B. $ 3
C. $ 4
D. $ 5

---

www.dos.pa.gov

The fee for taking an acknowledgment (each additional name) is _____.

A. $ 2
B. $ 3
C. $ 4
D. $ 5

---

www.dos.pa.gov

The fee for administering oath or affirmation (per individual taking oath or affirmation) is _____.

A. $ 2
B. $ 3
C. $ 4
D. $ 5

ANSWERS

D. 5
(www.dos.pa.gov)

The fee for taking an acknowledgment is **$ 5.**

A. $ 2
(www.dos.pa.gov)

The fee for taking an acknowledgment (each additional name) is **$ 2**

D. $ 5
(www.dos.pa.gov)

The fee for administering oath or affirmation (per individual taking oath or affirmation) is **$ 5**.

ACE THE PENNSYLVANIA NOTARY PUBLIC EXAM

MULTIPLE CHOICE QUESTIONS

---

www.dos.pa.gov

The fee for taking verification on oath or affirmation (no matter how many signatures) is _____.

A. $ 2
B. $ 3
C. $ 4
D. $ 5

---

www.dos.pa.gov

The fee for witnessing or attesting a signature (per signature) is _____.

A. $ 2
B. $ 3
C. $ 4
D. $ 5

---

www.dos.pa.gov

The fee for certifying or attesting a copy or deposition (per certified copy) is _____.

A. $ 2
B. $ 3
C. $ 4
D. $ 5

ANSWERS

D. $ 5
(www.dos.pa.gov)

The fee for taking verification on oath or affirmation (no matter how many signatures) is **$ 5**.

D. $ 5
(www.dos.pa.gov)

The fee for witnessing or attesting a signature (per signature) is **$ 5**.

D. $ 5
(www.dos.pa.gov)

The fee for certifying or attesting a copy or deposition (per certified copy) is **$ 5**.

ACE THE PENNSYLVANIA NOTARY PUBLIC EXAM

MULTIPLE CHOICE QUESTIONS

www.dos.pa.gov

The fee for noting a protest of a negotiable instrument (per page) is _____.

A. $ 2
B. $ 3
C. $ 4
D. $ 5

---

www.dos.pa.gov

Notaries may charge fees as set by _____.

A. the county clerk
B. the register of deeds
C. the Pennsylvania State Comptroller
D. the Department of State

---

www.dos.pa.gov

Fees may be _____ by notaries

A. doubled
B. waived
C. increased
D. tripled

ANSWERS

B. $ 3
(www.dos.pa.gov)

The fee for noting a protest of a negotiable instrument (per page) is **$ 3**.

D. the Department of State
(www.dos.pa.gov)

Notaries may charge fees as set by the **Department of State**.

B. waived
(www.dos.pa.gov)

Fees may be **waived** by notaries.

ACE THE PENNSYLVANIA NOTARY PUBLIC EXAM

MULTIPLE CHOICE QUESTIONS

Which of the following does not appear on the official stamp of a notary public?
A. The words "Commonwealth of Pennsylvania – Notary Seal."
B. The date of birth of the notary public.
C. The name as it appears on the commission of the notary and the words "Notary Public."
D. The name of the county in which the notary public maintains an office.

Which of the following does not appear on the official stamp of a notary public?
A. The date the notary's current commission expires.
B. The seven-digit commission identification number assigned by the Department.
C. The words "Notary Public."
D. The date the notary's current commission commenced.

Which of the following statements is not correct?
A. No words or terms on the official stamp may be abbreviated.
B. The official stamp or notary seal shall be stamped or affixed to the notarial certificate near the notary's signature or attached to or logically associated with an electronic record containing the notary's signature.
C. A notary public may place an imprint of the notary's official stamp over any signature in a record to be notarized or over any writing in a notarial certificate.
D. A notary public shall not alter or deface the official stamp.

ANSWERS

B. The date of birth of the notary public.
(RULONA Regulations 167.21)

D. The date the notary's current commission commenced.
(RULONA Regulations 167.21)

C. is not correct.
(RULONA Regulations 167.21)

A notary public shall NOT place an imprint of the notary's official stamp over any signature in a record to be notarized or over any writing in a notarial certificate.

ACE THE PENNSYLVANIA NOTARY PUBLIC EXAM

MULTIPLE CHOICE QUESTIONS

Which of the following statements is not correct?
A. Notary public may use an embossed or crimped image in the performance of a notarial act.
B. Use of embosser can be only in conjunction with the use of an official stamp.
C. Embosser cannot be placed over signature or printed material.
D. Notary public may use any other notary public's embosser or any other object in lieu of the notary public's official stamp to perform a notarial act.

Which of the following is not correct? A notary journal must contain:
A. The name of the notary public as it appears on his birth certificate.
B. The notary public's commission number;
C. The notary public's commission expiration date;
D. The notary public's office address of record with the Department;

Which of the following is not correct? A notary journal must contain:

A. Statement that in the event of death of the notary public, journal shall be delivered or mailed to the office of the recorder of deeds in the country where the notary last maintained an office;
B. The meaning of any not commonly abbreviated word or symbol used in recording a notarial act in the notarial journal;
C. The signature of the notary public;
D. A copy of the will of the notary public.

ANSWERS

D is not correct. It should read:

Notary public **shall not** use any other notary public's embosser or any other object in lieu of the notary public's official stamp to perform a notarial act.
(RULONA Regulations 167.23)

A is not correct. It should read:

A. The name of the notary public as it appears **on the commission**.
(RULONA Regulations 167.31)

D. A copy of the will of the notary public.
(RULONA Regulations 167.31)

This is not a requirement.

MULTIPLE CHOICE QUESTIONS

Which of the following is <u>not</u> correct? Prohibited entries in a notary public journal include an individual's first name or first initial and last name in combination with and linked to any one or more of the following data elements when the data elements are not encrypted or redacted:
A. Social Security number.
B. Driver's license number
C. Financial account number, credit or debit card number, with any required security code or access code
D. The fee paid by the receiver of the notarial service.

Which of the following is <u>not</u> correct?
Records for which a notary may not issue a certified copy include:
A. Vital Records (birth and death certificates)
B. U.S. Naturalization Certificates
C. Any government-issued record which on its face states "do not copy," or "illegal to copy" etc.
D Any record which is allowed by law to copy or certify

Which of the following is correct?
Records for which a notary may not issue a certified copy include:
A. Private records, leases
B. Drivers' licenses, Transcripts, Bills of sale
C. Diplomas, Contracts, medical records
D. U.S. Naturalization Certificates

ANSWERS

D. The fee paid by the receiver of the notarial service.
(RULONA Regulations 167.32)

D is not correct because it is not one of the items listed in this section and is a required notation.

D is not correct

This should read:
D. Any record which is **prohibited** by law to copy or certify.
(RULONA Regulations 167.65)

D. U.S. Naturalization Certificates

Notaries may **NOT** issue a certified copy of a U.S. Naturalization Certificate. Therefore, the answer is D.
(RULONA Regulations 167.65)

ACE THE PENNSYLVANIA NOTARY PUBLIC EXAM

Practice Test 1

1. The jurisdiction of notaries appointed by the Secretary of the Commonwealth is:
A. county of residence only.
B. only the county where the business of the notary is located.
C. the Commonwealth.
D. the US states.

2. If a notary changes his office address within the Commonwealth, notice in writing or electronically shall be given to the Secretary and the recorder of deeds of the county of original appointment by the notary within _____ days of such change.
A. 5
B. 10
C. 20
D. 30

3. Which of the following is not correct? Prohibited entries in a notary public journal include an individual's first name or first initial and last name in combination with and linked to any one or more of the following data elements when the data elements are not encrypted or redacted:
A. Social Security number.
B. Driver's license number
C. Financial account number, credit or debit card number, with any required security code or access code
D. The fee paid by the receiver of the notarial service.

4. Which of the following is not correct?
A notary is not required to use an electronic seal, if the following information is attached to the electronic signature or electronic record being notarized, acknowledged or verified:
A. The full name of the notary along with the words "Notary Public."
B. The name of the county in which the notary maintains an office.
C. The date the notary's commission is due to expire.
D. The brand name of the electronic device being employed.

275

5. The jurisdiction of notaries public is coextensive with the boundaries of the _____.
A. Commonwealth
B. North America
C. Commonwealth and Canada
D. county where principal office is located

6. Which of the following is not correct?
A. A notarial certificate has to be executed at the same time as the performance of the notarial act.
B. A notarial certificate must be signed and dated by the notarial officer.
C. A notarial certificate must identify the county and state in which the notarial act is performed.
D. A notarial certificate must contain the date of birth of the notarial officer.

7. Which of the following is not correct?
"In a representative capacity" means a person is acting as:
A. an authorized officer or representative;
B. a public officer, or personal representative in the capacity stated in a record;
C. an authorized agent or attorney
D. an unauthorized representative.

8. The notary public bond, as well as the commission and oath of office, shall be recorded in the _____ of the county in which the notary maintains an office at the time of appointment or reappointment.
A. office of the chief clerk
B. comptroller's office
C. office of the recorder of deeds
D. fiduciary office

9. Which of the following is correct?
A. Notary public may allow his landlord to be responsible for the security of his stamping device.
B. Notary public may allow another individual to use the stamping device to perform a notarial act.
C. A journal may be created on a tangible medium only.
D. A journal and each public record of the notary public are exempt from execution.

10. A declaration made in front of a notary that the person signed the record for the reason stated in the record; and that if the person signed as a representative, he did so with proper authority is:
A. a conviction
B. a knowledgeable statement
C. a veritas oath
D. an acknowledgment

11. Which of the following is not listed as a notarial act in RULONA 302?
A. taking an acknowledgment
B. administering an oath or affirmation
C. notarizing the signature of the notary's wife
D. noting a protest of a negotiable instrument.

12. Within _____ days after appointment and before issuance of a commission as a notary public, the applicant must obtain a surety bond in the amount of $_____ or the amount set by regulation of the department.
A. 30....$15,000
B. 45....$10,000
C. 15....$15,000
D. 30....$10,000

13. Which of the following is not correct? A notarial act may be performed in this Commonwealth by:
A. A judge of a court of record.
B. A clerk, deputy clerk of a court having a seal.
C. A prothonotary.
D. Any banker of a US bank.

14. Which of the following is not correct? A notarial certificate:
A. must be executed contemporaneously with the performance of the notarial act;
B. be signed and dated by the notarial officer
C. must be on 8.5 X 11 size paper.
D. must contain the title of the notarial officer

15. If a notary resigns or his commission is revoked, he shall deliver the journal of the notary public to the office of the recorder of deeds in the county where the notary public last maintained an office within _____ days of resignation or revocation of commission.
A. 10
B. 30
C. 45
D. 60

16. An act which may result in sanctions of a notary public include conviction of any _____ or other specified offenses.
A. petty offense
B. misdemeanor
C. felony
D. transgression

17. A commission as a notary public authorizes notary public to:
A. assist persons in drafting legal records
B. give legal advice
C. practice law.
D. note protests of negotiable instruments

18. Persons serving with Armed Forces of the US or their dependents may acknowledge before any commissioned officer in active service of the armed forces of the US with the rank of _____ or higher.
A. Second Lieutenant
B. First Lieutenant
C. First Sergeant
D. Major

19. A notary surety bond ($10,000) is meant to protect:
A. the courts.
B. the Secretary of the Commonwealth.
C. the signers of the notarized paper.
D. the notary testing agency.

20. Which of the following is not correct?
A. The fee for taking verification on oath or affirmation (no matter how many signatures) is $ 5.
B. The fee for noting a protest of a negotiable instrument (per page) is $ 3
C. The fee for taking an acknowledgment (each additional name) is $ 2.
D. The fee for certifying or attesting a copy or deposition (per certified copy) is $ 2.

21. If an applicant's preferred signature is not legible and recognizable, the applicant must also legibly print his or her name immediately adjacent to his or her preferred signature. The preceding statement is true:
A. Only if the notary has a disability.
B. In all cases.
C. Only if notary does not charge a fee for the notarial service.
D. Only if the notary is over the age of 62.

22. A notary public who wishes to perform notarial acts with respect to electronic records shall be authorized by the _____ to act as an "electronic notary" or "e-notary" prior to performing notarial acts with respect to electronic records.
A. county clerk
B. register of deeds
C. chief judge
D. Department

23. In acting as a notary public, a notary shall sign the notary's name exactly and only as it appears on the _____ or otherwise execute the notary's electronic signature in a manner that attributes such signature to the notary public identified on the commission.
A. birth certificate
B. social security card
C. notary public commission
D. graduation certificate

24. If a notarial act relates to a statement made in or a signature executed on a record, person making statement or executing signature shall appear _____ before the notary.
A. by telephone
B. text message
C. by video conference
D. personally

25. A notary public shall maintain a journal in which the notary public records in _____ order all notarial acts that the notary public performs.
A. his preferred
B. chronological
C. alphabetical
D. limit

26. The department may impose an administrative penalty of up to $_____ on a notary public for each act or omission which constitutes a violation of RULONA.
A. $ 250
B. $ 500
C. $ 750
D. $ 1,000

27. A notary may:
A. charge any fee
B. charge only statutory fee amounts
C. not waive a fee.
D. not charge a fee to ambulance drivers.

28. Which of the following is not correct?
"Conviction" as per RULONA 302 means any of the following, even if a sentence was not ordered by a court:
A. An entry of a plea of guilty or "no contest".
B. A guilty verdict in a trial (with or without a jury).
C. A finding of not guilty due to insanity, or guilty but mentally ill.
D. A verdict of not guilty.

29. If a notary public applicant is not a resident of Pennsylvania, the applicant:
A. must be a resident of New York or New Jersey.
B. must have a relative residing in Pennsylvania.
C. must have a place of employment or practice in this Commonwealth.
D. must have a post office box number address in the Commonwealth.

30. Which of the following is not correct?
Generally, a notary journal may not contain the:
A. personal financial information about the client.
B. first or last name of the client.
C. complete social security number of a client.
D. complete driver's license number of the client.

ANSWERS: PRACTICE EXAM #1

1. C....Notary Public Law : Section 2
2. A....Notary Public Law: Section 7
3. D....RULONA Regulations 167.32
4. D....Notary Public Law: Section 12
5. A....Notary Public Law: Section 2
6. D....RULONA 315
7. D....RULONA 302
8. C   Notary Public Law: Section 9
9. D....RULONA 319
10. D   RULONA 302
11. C   RULONA 302
12. B   RULONA 321)
13. D   RULONA 310
14. C   RULONA 315
15. B   RULONA 319
16. C   RULONA 323
17. D   RULONA Regulations 167.66
18. A   Uniform Acknowledgment Act: Section 10.0
19. C   Notary Public Law: Section 8
20. D   http://www.dos.pa.gov: fee schedule
21. B   RULONA regulations 167.14(d)
22. D   RULONA Regulations 167.81
23. C   Notary Public Law: Section 9
24. D   RULONA 306
25. B   RULONA 319
26. D   RULONA 323
27. B   Notary Public Law: Section 21
28. D   RULONA 302
29. C   RULONA Regulations 167.11
30. B   RULONA Regulations 167.21

ACE THE PENNSYLVANIA NOTARY PUBLIC EXAM

Practice Test 2

1. Which of the following is eligible to hold the office of notary public?
A. judge of the Supreme Court of Pennsylvania.
B. member of Congress.
C. the head of a Pennsylvania state department
D. a store owner who qualifies for the office

2. Which of the following is not correct? A notary journal must contain:
A. Statement that in the event of death of the notary public, journal shall be delivered or mailed to the office of the recorder of deeds in the country where the notary last maintained an office;
B. The meaning of any not commonly abbreviated word or symbol used in recording a notarial act in the notarial journal;
C. The signature of the notary public;
D. A copy of the will of the notary public.

3. The fee for witnessing or attesting a signature (per signature) is _____.
A. $ 2
B. $ 3
C. $ 4
D. $ 5

4. Which of the following is correct?
Notaries have power to:
A. adjust the amount of their statutory fees.
B. administer oaths and affirmations.
C. adjudge a person in contempt.
D. interrogate a witness during trial.

5. Any person who is a notary public and who resides outside this Commonwealth shall be deemed to have irrevocably appointed the _____ as the person's agent upon whom may be served any summons, subpoena, order or other process.
A. clerk of the county
B. public attorney
C. Comptroller of the Commonwealth
D. Secretary of the Commonwealth

6. Notaries may charge fees as set by _____.
A. the county clerk
B. the register of deeds
C. the Pennsylvania State Comptroller
D. the Department of State

7. The official notary signature shall be registered, in the "Notary Register" in the prothonotary's office of county where the notary maintains an office, within ____ days after appointment or reappointment.
A. 10
B. 15
C. 30
D. 45

8. If a notary public fails to give a bond and cause the bond and the commission and oath to be recorded within ____ days after the beginning of the term, his commission shall be null and void.
A. 15
B. 30
C. 45
D. 60

9. Which of the following does not appear on the official stamp of a notary public?
A. the date the notary's current commission expires
B. the seven-digit commission identification number assigned by the Department
C. the words "Notary Public"
D. the date the notary's current commission commenced.

10. Satisfactory evidence includes all of the following, except:
A. a US passport that is not expired
B. a driver's license not expired
C. nondriver state identification card not expired
D. a credit card not expired

11. Which of the following do not apply to the official stamp of a notary public?
A. The words "Commonwealth of Pennsylvania"
B. The word "USA"
C. County where notary public maintains his office.
D. Date notary public's commission expires.

12. The official signature of each notary public shall be registered, for a fee of 50¢, in the "Notary Register" provided for that purpose in the _____ office of the county where the notary public maintains an office.
A. fiscal
B. prothonotary
C. tax
D. Secretary of the Commonwealth

13. A notary public may advertise or represent that the notary public:
A. may assist persons in drafting legal records.
B. may give legal advice.
C. is a "notario".
D. may certify copies of depositions.

14. An acknowledgment of a married woman:
A. must be made with husband's consent.
B. may be made in same form as though she were unmarried.
C. must be prepared in duplicate.
D. must be witnessed by two witnesses.

15. The fee for taking an acknowledgment is:
A. $ 2
B. $ 3
C. $ 5
D. $ 7

16. The seal shall have a maximum height of _____, inches with a plain border.
A. (.5) inch and width of two and one-half (2 1/2)
B. (1.5) inch and width of three and one-half (3 1/2)
C. (1) inch and width of three and one-half (3 1/2)
D. (2) inch and width of four and one-half (4 1/2)

17. When may a notary public charge any fee for notarizing the supporting affidavit required in an Emergency Absentee Ballot or the affidavit of a person needing assistance to vote an absentee ballot?
A. When the resident is not outside the county of residence.
B. When the person is not eligible due to high income.
C. Under certain circumstances relating to party affiliation.
D. Under no circumstances.

18. Which of the following will be accepted on the application or as part of the signature required on a notarial act?
A. initials alone
B. nickname
C. prefixes such a "Doctor" or "Reverend'.
D. suffixes such as "Junior" or "Senior".

19. Applications for reappointment to the office of notary public shall be filed at least ___ months prior to the expiration of the commission under which the notary is acting.
A. 2
B. 3
C. 4
D. 6

20. If a notary public performs a notarial act in which he has a pecuniary interest in the transaction, the notarial act is _____.
A. financially sound
B. monetarily recorded
C. permissible
D. voidable

21. A notarial certificate must be executed:
A. 24 hours before the acknowledgment.
B. contemporaneously with the performance of the notarial act.
C. in front of 2 witnesses.
D. with malintent.

22. Before a notary performs the initial notarial act with respect to an electronic record, a notary public shall notify the _____ that the notary will be performing notarial acts with respect to electronic records and identify each technology the notary intends to use.
A. county clerk
B. chief clerk
C. county assessor
D. department

ACE THE PENNSYLVANIA NOTARY PUBLIC EXAM

23. If a notarial act relates to a statement made in or a signature executed on a record, person making statement or executing signature shall appear _____ before the notary.
A. electronically
B. by phone
C. personally
D. in absentia

24. A notary public who is not an attorney may not use the terms_____ or _____.
A. notary public or notary
B. "notario" or "notario publico"
C. notary or notary public
D. none of the above

25. Which of the following statements is not correct?
A. Notary public may use an embossed or crimped image in the performance of a notarial act.
B. Use of embosser can be only in conjunction with the use of an official stamp.
C. Embosser cannot be placed over signature or printed material.
D. Notary public may use any other notary public's embosser or any other object in lieu of the notary public's official stamp to perform a notarial act.

26. The bond, commission and oath of office, shall be recorded in the _____ in which the notary maintains an office at the time of appointment or reappointment.
A. the office of the Secretary
B. the tax office of the county
C. office of the recorder of deeds of the county
D. the fiscal office

27. The fee for noting a protest of a negotiable instrument (per page) is _____.
A. $ 2
B. $ 3
C. $ 4
D. $ 5

28. A notarial act shall be evidenced by:
A. a sworn affidavit in duplicate
B. a certus priori
C. a certificate
D. two witnesses

29. The failure of a notarial officer to perform a duty or meet a requirement specified in this chapter:
A. invalidates a notarial act performed by the notarial officer.
B. immediately voids a notarial act performed by the notarial officer.
C. immediately makes null a notarial act performed by the notarial officer.
D. does not invalidate a notarial act performed by the notarial officer.

30. Notaries:
A. may charge clerical and administrative fees and customers should be informed prior to notarization.
B. may not charge clerical and administrative fees.
C. may charge notarial fees up to three times the statutory amounts.
D. may not charge fees to persons receiving public assistance.

ANSWERS: PRACTICE EXAM # 2

1. D   Notary Public Law: Section 4
2. D   RULONA Regulations 167.31
3. D   www.dos.pa.gov
4. B   Notary Public Law: Section 16
5. D   Notary Public Law: Section 3
6. D   www.dos.pa.gov
7. D   Notary Public Law: Section 9
8. C   Notary Public Law: Section 8
9. D   RULONA Regulations 167.21
10. D   RULONA 307
11. B   RULONA 317
12. B   RULONA 321
13. D   RULONA 325
14. B   Uniform Acknowledgment Act: Section 6
15. C   http://www.dos.pa.gov: fee schedule
16. C   Notary Public Law: Section 12
17. D   RULONA Regulations 161.2
18. D   RULONA Regulations 167.41
19. A   Notary Public Law: Section 6
20. D   RULONA: Section 304
21. B   RULONA 315
22. D   RULONA 320
23. C   RULONA 306
24. B   RULONA 325
25. D   RULONA Regulations 167.23
26. C   Notary Public Law: Section 9
27. B   www.dos.pa.gov
28. C   RULONA 315
29. D   (RULONA 326)
30. A   http://www.dos.pa.gov

Made in the USA
Middletown, DE
06 August 2020